Cathy Burkey

About the Author

Rick Carson is the creator of the renowned Gremlin-Taming Method™. He is the author of three HarperCollins books, including this one. His seminal work, *Taming Your Gremlin®: A Guide to Enjoying Yourself,* has been in print for twenty years and has been translated into several languages.

Rick's work has influenced thousands in virtually every walk of life. For thirty years he has been a counselor, personal/executive coach, and trainer for mental health professionals, businesses, and non-profit organizations. His work is used in the training of psychotherapists, personal and executive coaches, substance abuse specialists, corrections personnel, teachers, corporate executives, and clergy. He is a former faculty member at the University of Texas Southwestern Medical School and a clinical member and approved supervisor for the American Association for Marriage and Family Therapy.

Rick is the founder and director of the Gremlin Taming Institute™ in Dallas. He and his wife, Leti, live in Colleyville, Texas. For more information visit www.tamingyourgremlin.com.

Taming
Your Gremlin®

REVISED EDITION

A Surprisingly Simple Method
for
Getting Out of Your Own Way

Rick Carson

Quill

An Imprint of HarperCollins*Publishers*

HarperCollins books may be purchased for educational, business, or sales promotional use. For information please write: Special Markets Department, HarperCollins Publishers Inc., 10 East 53rd Street, New York, NY 10022.

First Quill edition published 2003.

Designed by Nancy B. Field

Illustrations by Novle Rogers

Library of Congress Cataloging-in-Publication Data

Carson, Richard David.
  Taming your gremlin : a surprisingly simple method for getting out of your own way / Rick Carson — Rev. ed.
      p. cm.
   ISBN 0-06-052022-1
   1. Happiness. 2. Success—Psychological aspects.
3. Self-perception. 4. Choice (Psychology). I. Title

BF575.H27C38 2003
158.1—dc21   2002191925

03 04 05 06 07 ❖ / RRD 10 9 8 7 6 5 4 3

In memory of
my mother, Eva,
my dad, Alex,
and
my brother, Frank,
with love

Acknowledgments

My mother, Eva, my dad, Al, and my brother, Frank, had a good thing going when they welcomed me into the environment of love and acceptance they were already enjoying. I felt safe and free there with them, and this fact of my existence seems somehow basic to my having the perspective offered in this book.

Being able to rely on love, loyalty, and friendship comes in handy anytime. This is especially true when faced with making a living, the illness and death of loved ones, and a publisher's deadline all at the same time. I'm deeply grateful to my wife, Leti, and our son, Jonah—the man I most admire.

Nancy Ferguson and I have been friends and colleagues for many years. She is a true manifestation of love and authenticity, and a gift to every human, cat, and dog fortunate enough to cross her path. The ease with which she lives the truth of who she is makes doing so easier for me. Nancy's friendship, hard work, and support of me and what I have to say are in great part why it's getting said.

To Novle Rogers, whose illustrations embellish both this and the original edition of *Taming Your Gremlin*®, I offer a West Texas, buddy-to-buddy sock on the arm. His art's got heart.

My colleague Jane Massengill phoned her way into my life two years ago. A marvelously talented gremlin-tamer in her own right, Jane has a dream of making certain every child on the planet learns Gremlin-Taming. If it can be done, Jane will do it. She's embraced the Gremlin-Taming Method™ in her own life and in her work, and her creativity and support have been inspiring to me. I'm pleased to have Jane as Director of the Gremlin Taming Institute™.

And I want to thank my friend Doug Rucker. He is a richly creative man with an extraordinary talent for envisioning possibilities and turning them into high-functioning realities. I'm grateful for the opportunity to be associated with Doug, his partner Jan Deatherage, and their unique and wonderful firm R & D Thinktank. Doug encouraged this project and the Gremlin Taming Institute™ from the beginning, and his input has been invaluable.

Teachers teach better when their students are eager. The way my friends, colleagues, and advanced trainees Linda Doutre, Vicki James, and Shelly Vaughn have embraced my work warms my heart. Respected and powerful psychotherapists and teachers themselves, each has added their own special twist to the Gremlin-Taming Method™, enhancing it with their own life experience and gifts. Many have and will continue to benefit because of their talents. I'm proud as punch to know them, and humbled by their devotion to their craft and to Gremlin-Taming™.

Facilitating others to resolve tough inner challenges is a craft like no other. My officemate and good friend Stan Ferguson appreciates the craft as much as I do, and our conversations make us both better at what we do. I respect Stan's insightfulness and relish his humor. His presence makes my sometimes hectic pace more tolerable, and my life more enjoyable. For years Stan has encouraged me to do a *Taming Your Gremlin*® workbook. While this book you hold isn't a workbook per se, Stan's encouragement to provide interactive activities helped me decide to do so. I thank him.

This book is more effective because of the input of Toni Sciarra at HarperCollins. Toni took the time to understand what I have to teach, and the challenge of doing so with the written word. She's been a true partner in the process. Getting paired with Toni feels like a gift to me.

I want to thank my friend Kathy Ross for her straightforward comments on the first draft of this revised edition, and for being the wonderful soul she is. Why she hangs out with that stick-in-the-mud Sister Mary Perfect, I'll never understand.

Sally Anderson, a very special lady, took her time to give my rough draft a tough going-over. Her comments were thorough and right on, and I appreciate them and Sally very much.

For three years in the early '70s I did postgraduate training at a magical place in time called the Gestalt Institute of Chicago. Among the talented faculty were two people to whom I have heartfelt gratitude, Claire Ridker and Charlotte Rosner. They were skillful practitioners and teachers and, watching them, I learned the value of authenticity as the ultimate therapeutic tool.

Finally, and above all, I want to thank Maharaji for showing me the ultimate gift within, giving me the tools to connect with it, and for continuing to remind me to do so.

Contents

Introduction:
Before You Begin
This Book

If you are reading *Taming Your Gremlin*® for the first time, I'd like to welcome you with the same words I used to introduce Gremlin-Taming™ to my readers twenty years ago:

This book is not intended to guide you to enlightenment, to eternal bliss, or to riches. It will, however, help you to enjoy yourself more and more each day. It is simple and practical and I hope that reading it brings you much pleasure.

If you've arrived here already familiar with the original book, even if you've studied it and have practiced Gremlin-Taming for a long time, I believe the additions and changes in this new edition will take you to a deeper level in your use of the method.

Beginning this revised and expanded edition of *Taming Your Gremlin* felt like trying to French kiss over the telephone. There was so much I wanted to say to you, but all I had to say it with were these little words, and as we all know, *the word is not the thing, nor the description the described.* Experience is the best teacher, and experience has its own language—at least that's true from my experience. It's the difference between *knowing about* and really *knowing*.

So not only are you about to get information—a lot of it—but I've included more interactive exercises than in the original work, more chances for you to learn from the inside out. I've also added more illustrative vignettes—some from my own life—and created several opportunities for you to review and reflect on what you are learning as you are learning it. I think you'll find this new and revised edition to be exceedingly practical and immediately applicable.

Much of the correspondence I have received since 1983, when *Taming Your Gremlin* was first published, is from people who have been practicing the Gremlin-Taming Method for years, not only as a practical tool for enhancing their inner experience day to day, but also to maintain their emotional equilibrium during hard-to-handle and, in some cases, excruciatingly difficult circumstances.

There is a common thread in their communication that is reflected in these words from a reader: "When I first picked up *Taming Your Gremlin* I thought it would be a sweet little self-help book. Instead, I found a lifelong discipline that has revolutionized my inner life." Most have recognized that *gremlin* is far more than a metaphor for negative thoughts and that the Gremlin-Taming Method is not simply a matter of choosing positive over negative thinking. Rather, the *former* is the source of most personal strife and societal distress, and the *latter* is an elegantly streamlined process that lies at the heart of the quest for inner peace.

Gremlin-Taming is practical and it is powerful. It is a method for meeting the inner challenge that is inherent in every activity from climbing Mount Everest to getting a good night's sleep. Gremlin-Taming, in a phrase or three, is a graceful process for choosing light over darkness, good over evil (and boy, those terms are loaded for people), or better yet, the true love that sustains you over the fear that can destroy you. It's a meaty subject, to say the least, but one that is germane to having a fulfilling inner life and a peaceful interdependence with others. We are, after all, in this thing together. And while it may sound like a wispy platitude, there is no getting around the raw and simple truth that peace on earth does, indeed, begin within.

Between our birth and our death is a steady stream of precious moments leading you and me, thus far, to here. It's good to be here with you as we embark on another adventure in Gremlin-Taming.

Taming Your Gremlin®

I

The Essentials

YOU AND I

There you are in the midst of your unique configuration of props and players, drawing in these words through your eyes, and here I am, way over here in another time and place, doing my best to be in communion with you. Here we sit, you and I, wrapped up in our bodies, smashing to smithereens the boundaries of time and space.

Tame you SAY, Ha..We'll see about dis. Hmmm

But we're not our bodies. We're not. Our bodies are constantly changing masses of matter. As a matter of fact, if you're over 30, as we speak, your ears are getting bigger, your nose is getting longer, and the distance is shrinking from the bottom of your feet to the top of your head. Frightening, but so. Bodies change. My body has done so dramatically. A lean 165 pounds now, I used to weigh, and this is the astonishing truth, 7 pounds 8 ounces. We're not our bodies.

And we're not our personalities. Personalities are just networks of behaviors that emerge from a matrix of beliefs we hold about who we are.

And we're not our beliefs. Beliefs, even the noblest of them, are just opinions that we develop loyalty to, so that we can pretend that the world has at least a modicum of predictability. Doing so helps us feel safe. Ironically, we sometimes fight to defend our beliefs, creating anything but a safe situation.

So we're not our beliefs; we're not our personalities; we're not our bodies. And we're not our thoughts. We have thoughts. Positive thoughts and negative thoughts. Thoughts about the past and thoughts about the future. Boring thoughts and strange thoughts. But we're not our thoughts.

So, what of that thing you really are? That thing that has a body, a personality, beliefs, and thoughts, but is none of these? It has had hundreds of names applied to it. *Soul, spirit, prana, re, chi, ki, God*, the *primordial vibration*, to name a few. It doesn't matter what we call it, because no name can circle it. It existed before the word. I often refer to it as *true love*. But for our purposes, here and now, let's call it *life*. Your life. Your very own life, humming away inside of you at this moment.

YOUR LIFE

It's your life. It's not your mother's life, your father's life, your spouse's, your employer's, or your child's. It's your life. Your very own life. A gift to you directly from the creator of this whole shebang. It's the greatest gift you will ever receive, and you already have it.

And if that's not enough to fill you with pride and satisfaction, consider this bonus. Not only do you get your very own life, but, just because you arrived on the planet as a human being, you get the consciousness to appreciate your gift of life and to respond to it however you would like, moment to moment and day to day. Your ability to respond to your life is known as your *response ability*. But it's not always easy to respond to this life gracefully, in great part because of a vile, vicious, villainous, insufferable bully lurking in the shadows of your very own mind: your gremlin.

YOUR GREMLIN

You already have some sense of your gremlin, though perhaps you never have focused your awareness on him or labeled him. Your gremlin is the narrator in your head. He has influenced you since you came into this world, and he accompanies you throughout your entire existence. He's with you when you wake up in the morning and when you go to sleep at night. He tells you who and how you are, and he defines and interprets your every experience. He wants you to accept his interpretations as reality, and his goal, from moment to moment, day to day, is to squelch the natural, vibrant you within.

I'm not sure of the factors that contributed to the

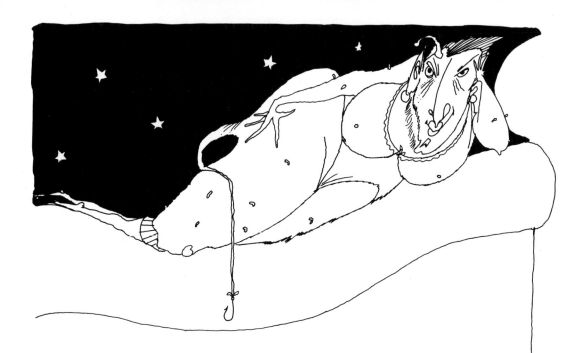

makeup of your particular gremlin. I am sure, however, that he uses some of your past experiences to hypnotize you into forming and living your life in accordance with self-limiting and sometimes frightening generalizations about you and what existence holds for you.

Your gremlin wants you to feel bad, and he carries out this loathsome pursuit via some sophisticated maneuvers, which we will discuss later, and by convincing you to waste time reliving the past, worrying about the future, and analyzing the relationships between all sorts of people and things. Your gremlin wants you to believe that he has your best interest at heart and that his primary purpose is to serve and protect you. His motive is actually much less honorable. He is intent on making you miserable.

Your gremlin's caution about life and living is inordinate and his methods of control are overzealous. He is not merely your inner critic or simply a part of your psychological makeup. Your gremlin is not your negative thoughts—he is the source of them. He is not your less-than-positive past experiences—he uses them. He is not your fears—he taunts you with them by creating the horror movie about your future that you sometimes watch.

He is your gremlin, and his personality, like his dastardly intention, is all his own. One thing is for certain. As you begin to *simply notice* your gremlin, you will become acutely sensitive to the fact that you are not your gremlin, but rather, his observer. You will see clearly that your gremlin has no real hold on you. As this awareness develops, you will begin to appreciate and enjoy your life more and more. It is for you, the observer, that this book is written.

THE NATURAL YOU (THE OBSERVER)

As I've said, your body will change over your lifetime. And your personality, too. And so will your opinions, your preferences, your performance style, and the various roles you play. The *natural you* is the one inside that miraculous mass of matter out of which you are now peering. The *natural me* is inside my own body, which is at this moment holding a pen. From inside this aging sculpture of hair, eyes, teeth, and limbs, the *natural me* is writing the words, "Hello in there."

You just pulled in through your eyes the words, "Hello in there."

The *natural you* understands the essence of my words. Your mind is busy making sense out of them. Your gremlin, meanwhile, is gnashing his teeth and screeching something like "This is ridiculous!" He's threatened by our relationship and threatened even more by the calling forth of the *natural you*—the *observer*—and he will do all in his power to bully or smooth-talk you off the path to clarity and simple contentment. He would love to convince you to trust him instead of trusting the uncontaminated experiences and observations of the *natural you*.

Your gremlin knows that way back when you were a pretty unsophisticated, funny-looking rookie at this game of life, the *natural you* learned complex tasks like walking and talking, and did so without an iota of knowledge about physics or kinesiology. Your gremlin knows that the *natural you* is wise, pristinely pure, and sharp as a tack, and that the *natural you* holds the key to your happiness. To seduce you away from trusting yourself, your gremlin will try to get you to dissect and analyze the meaning of these words. If you follow his lead and do so, you might get bored or confused. It's no big deal if this happens. Confusion is just your brain reacting to your gremlin's demand that you fit what you're reading into your brain's preconceived ideas *about* what you're reading. Your gremlin wants you to feel suspicious, anxious, hopeless, and ultimately empty.

The *natural you*, on the other hand, is the source of simple satisfaction. Known also as the *observer*, the natural you is a pro at integrating wisdom and eliminating bunk.

Your gremlin is probably, at this very moment, beginning to go wild. Your gremlin's sole purpose is to divert you from finding the simple pleasure inside of you, and his (or her) job is a lot easier when he can hide outside of your awareness. He hates that I'm exposing him. Hear his chatter, but don't take it too seriously. He might say something like:

"You've got more important things to do.
Get busy."

or

"You're just going to get your hopes up and end up
disappointed. Nothing's going to change, least of all
you, Babycakes."

or

"Schmuck! You need another self-help book like
you need a hole in the head."

Well, he's wrong on all counts. Again, hear his chatter, but don't take it too seriously. Simply notice it. Then make a choice to direct your awareness back to these words, back to your gremlin, or elsewhere. *Awareness* and *choice* are the primary elements of *simply noticing*.

SIMPLY NOTICING

The *simply* in *simply noticing* cannot be overstated. *Simply noticing* has nothing to do with predicting the future, undoing the past, analyzing, or intellectually understanding anything. *Simply noticing* involves only simply noticing. That is, paying attention—the same sort of attention you would pay to a good movie. When you watch a good movie, you simply let yourself be entertained. You don't work at enjoying the movie. You just cast your awareness on the screen and let the movie do its thing. By the same token, if you're talking to the person next to you throughout the film or are mired in some other mental activity, you miss the movie. Simply noticing requires effort. It does not require strain.

EFFORT AND STRAIN

Jimmy Baker was on my flag football team when we were fifth graders at Overton Elementary in Lubbock, Texas. We were the Overton Oxens. (Okay, okay, it should have been *oxen*, but hey—we were in elementary school.) Our coach, Mr. Tyrell, knew that the keys to turning the Overton Oxens into a winning squad were speed and inspiration. He attempted to ensure the latter by calling us "men," letting us put black gunk under our eyes, and telling us daily that, "It's not the size of the dog in the fight, it's the size of the fight in the dog." Jimmy Baker and I had total faith in Coach Tyrell (though our faith took a minor dip the day Coach bellowed at the top of his lungs, "All right, men, pair off in threes!").

To get us up to snuff on the speed thing, Coach Tyrell used to shout simply "Go!" and wave his right arm over his head in a circular motion. With this cue from him we screamed, "Oxens, oxens, oxens!" and started running around the football field. We did this almost every day of the season, and miraculously, most of us got faster. We each developed our own method of running. I learned to run on the balls of my feet, and Lee Jason, our quick and feisty quarterback, unclenched his fists when he ran, pointing his fingers out like karate guys do. He said it helped him cut through the air. Jimmy Baker's approach to becoming a speedster was to stomp the ground fast and hard as he ran.

The intensity of Jimmy's stomps increased in direct proportion to his ever-heightening desire to run faster. He huffed, puffed, and sweated with undaunted zeal. His desire was inspiring, but his pace remained deplorable. The harder Jimmy stomped, the slower he got. Having witnessed Jimmy's frustration and that of others since,

I'm sure, just as sure as I'm sitting here, that one can't run faster by stomping the ground harder. Certainly there are times when gutting up comes in handy, but all in all, toil dominated by tension is bad for your health and your disposition, and won't help you do a quicker or better job.

That's the difference between effort and strain. When it comes to *simply noticing*, and ultimately to taming your gremlin, the former applies and the latter impedes. The kind of effort involved in *simply noticing* will be helpful right here and now, in our relationship—yours and mine.

As you read on, trust the *natural you* inside that body of yours—the one behind your concepts and preconceived notions, the one deeper than your personality and identity, to *simply notice* these words. You need not try to figure out anything. *Simply notice* and make a choice to read on or to stop for a while. Either way is fine. As for me, I'm here for the long haul and what I have to offer is here for you to enjoy at your leisure. In other words, where our relationship is concerned, your part is to show up, relax, and gently pay attention. My part is to wait right here and save your place.

But *simply noticing* has benefits way beyond our relationship. *Simply noticing* is the disarmingly potent first step in the Gremlin-Taming Method. As you refine it, you will actually be able to observe not just what is going on around you, but your own thoughts, emotions, memories, and fantasies in the very moment they are occurring. Doing so kicks into play an age-old, infallible, and powerful process sometimes known as the Zen Theory of Change.

THE ZEN THEORY OF CHANGE

Here is my paraphrased version of the theory:

I free myself not by trying to be free, but by *simply noticing* how I am imprisoning myself in the very moment I am imprisoning myself.

It's been said lots of ways by lots of people. Over 2,500 years ago Lao Tzu brushed with picture symbols the *Tao Te Ching*, which included this wisdom:

Simply notice the natural order of things.
Work with it rather than against it.
For to try to change what is only sets up resistance.

Lao Tzu was a smart cookie.

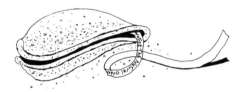

TRYING AND FIGURING OUT

I hope that you will not try to figure out the gist of what I am saying. To *try* and/or *figure out* is to invite your gremlin into our relationship. Two is company and three is a crowd, especially if the third party is a gremlin. Besides, what I have to say to you is none of his business. Instead of *trying* and/or *figuring out*, simply relax and breathe comfortably, simply noticing what you are reading. If you get bored, confused, overwhelmed, distracted, or spaced out, simply stop for a while.

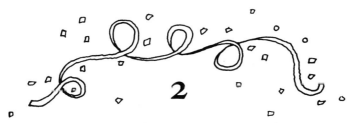

2

More About Gremlins

Gremlins are very sophisticated and have developed elaborate styles of blocking the natural, excited, vibrant soul within each of us. As you increase your awareness of your own gremlin, you may actually develop some appreciation for his creativity. My choice to use a male pronoun in general reference to gremlins grows out of my very intimate (not to be confused with enjoyable) relationship with my own gremlin, who most often presents himself as a male. I say "most often" because gremlins change not only their gender but their entire personality from moment to moment and from situation to situation.

Your gremlin can appear as your best friend and adviser, or as your grossest and most ill-intentioned enemy. Regardless of his appearance, he must be observed. Left to carry out his own will, he will make you miserable. He might allow you occasional highs, but most often he will lead you into periods of intense anxiety, sadness, anger, and eventually emptiness.

GREMLINS I HAVE MET

Many of my clients, students, and trainees have come to know their gremlins so well that they have developed their abilities to visualize them. They tell me that this has been an aid in helping them to tame their gremlins.

A few of the gremlins my clients have introduced me to are described below. Your gremlin may resemble any or all of these, but I assure you that his style of making you miserable will be unique. After all, he has known you for years and has developed sophisticated maneuvers for squelching the natural you within.

Gremlins are far more complex than these few examples indicate. Those I have met have had an impressive repertoire of methods for engendering misery. Each, however, seems to have a preferred strategy.

The General

When I met Jack he was 32. He was a financially successful attorney whose battles with his gremlin had saddled him with an array of stress-related symptoms and ailments. He described his gremlin as short, stout, bald, straight-backed, and wearing a military uniform. His gremlin insisted that Jack lead life in accordance with a complex scheme of rules, regulations, shoulds, and ought tos. He had Jack clearly convinced that were it not for his advice, Jack would be a sluglike, ineffectual mama's boy. Jack had big biceps, a black belt in karate, and an inability to get an erection.

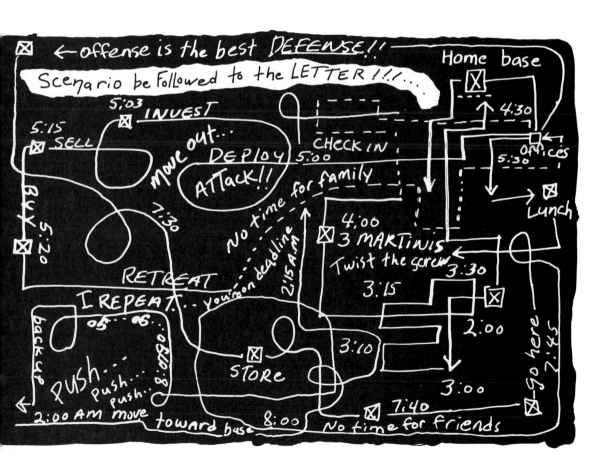

The Artist

Joseph was 40 when we met. He was a successful research psychologist whose gremlin had him convinced that unless his (the gremlin's) advice was followed, Joseph would eventually become destitute and lonely. From time to time, Joseph's gremlin showed him a beautiful painting entitled *Joseph Leading a Happy Life*. He convinced Joseph that fulfillment, happiness, and general comfort with himself would result once Joseph had arranged his circumstances and his life into a living version of the beautiful painting.

As Joseph began to *simply notice* the Artist, he also noticed that the Artist was continually altering the composition of the beautiful painting. He further noticed that the Artist usually modified the painting about the time Joseph got close to matching his life to the painting. This left Joseph feeling somewhat like the proverbial horse that follows the carrot. When Joseph sought me out, he was taking his third postdoctoral psychology residency and was considering suicide.

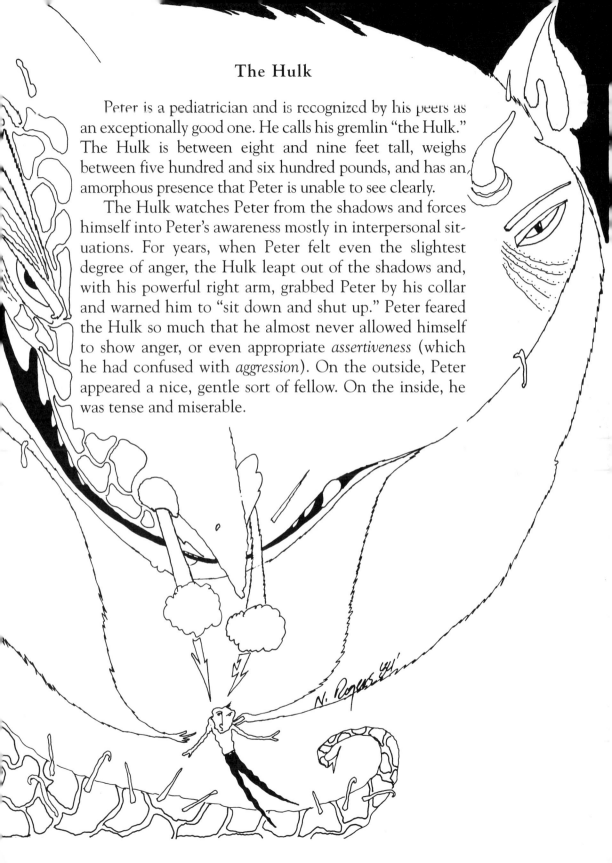

The Hulk

Peter is a pediatrician and is recognized by his peers as an exceptionally good one. He calls his gremlin "the Hulk." The Hulk is between eight and nine feet tall, weighs between five hundred and six hundred pounds, and has an amorphous presence that Peter is unable to see clearly.

The Hulk watches Peter from the shadows and forces himself into Peter's awareness mostly in interpersonal situations. For years, when Peter felt even the slightest degree of anger, the Hulk leapt out of the shadows and, with his powerful right arm, grabbed Peter by his collar and warned him to "sit down and shut up." Peter feared the Hulk so much that he almost never allowed himself to show anger, or even appropriate *assertiveness* (which he had confused with *aggression*). On the outside, Peter appeared a nice, gentle sort of fellow. On the inside, he was tense and miserable.

The Big Shot

The last time I encountered my gremlin was about two minutes ago. A big man, mid-60s, he looks wealthy and flashy—black suit, diamond pinky ring, smoking a big cigar. His theme today is something like, "You're a nobody, kid." He was pontificating with great confidence about how HarperCollins would quickly relegate this book to the backlist and within a week or two respond to my inquiries with a "Rick who? Gremlin what?" He threw in some tidbits about age, a few "it's now or never" scare tactics, and something about starvation and complete worthlessness. When I brought him into the light so I could simply notice him, he shrank and became a whiny, pudgy, fat guy wearing a diaper.

I'm certainly no master of Gremlin-Taming, but I am a conscientious student, and have been since I developed this process nearly 30 years ago. One thing I can absolutely attest to is that the method not only works, it's progressive. In other words, as you practice, you're going to get better and better at using it under tougher and tougher circumstances and at applying it easily and swiftly. Simply noticing is just the first tool in a three-tiered process, but it is a powerful tool that you will steadily use more skillfully through practice. The potential is literally boundless.

Each time you tame your gremlin on the spot, the natural you will come out and take over. You will begin to learn experientially, not just cognitively, the power of the Gremlin-Taming process and of the natural you. As a result, you will develop a bone-deep self-trust and a confidence in your Gremlin-Taming abilities.

Your gremlin is not going to give up trying to nail you. That's his job. But you'll be so confident in your ability to tame him that even an all-out assault will seem inconsequential and hardly worth your attention. So practice.

HEY You!! And You Too!! Give Me Fifty.

Coach Don Ledup

Dale was a well-established software salesman when I met him. He was extremely handsome, a hard worker, and wealthy (because of his hard work). When we initially came in contact, he worked so hard and moved so fast that I was surprised he found the time to put so many things in his mouth. Dale smoked two packages of cigarettes a day, had two or three martinis at lunch, and drank several cocktails every evening. When I told Dale he would not be allowed to smoke during our time together, his gremlin raised his head in fury. This gave Dale and me an opportunity to *simply notice* him.

Subsequently, Dale labeled his gremlin "Coach Don Ledup." Coach Don Ledup resembled a coach I once had.

17

Most of the coaches I have had have been either big and burly or little and feisty. Dale's gremlin reminded me of the little and feisty variety. I don't recall ever seeing my feisty coach walk or sit. He was always running around. As he ran he would shout things like, "Lotta hustle, gang," or "Go, go, go," or "Be number one." Sometimes he would just yell noises like "Hubba, hubba, hubba." He never made much sense, but he had a knack for getting people moving. As a matter of fact, it was almost impossible to be still when you were around him. Dale's gremlin was very much like this coach.

Dale saw Coach Don Ledup as having a whistle around his neck, as being short, thin, strong, and not so much fast as quick. He used the same sort of words that my feisty coach used, with emphasis on the "Be number one!" For years he had Dale convinced that the world was a race and that Dale absolutely had to win it. Dale was so busy running the race that he never took the time to experience the world for himself. His coach spent so much time yelling at him in his loud, speedy voice that Dale seldom observed what was going on around him. He simply took the coach's word that he was in the middle of a race that he needed to win, and he just kept running. Somewhere in the process he learned to drink alcohol and smoke cigarettes, and he tended to do these things with the same fervor with which he ran the race.

One of the myths that Dale's coach perpetuated was that there was a positive correlation between Dale feeling harried and his attaining the monetary status he desired. He convinced Dale that in order to move at a productive and efficient pace in his work, he must feel speedy and somewhat frenetic on the inside.

Reverend Al Drydup

Lucille was 35 when I first met her. Her gremlin looked like her grandfather, only he wore a clerical collar and engaged her by preaching to her. He especially liked to make appearances when Lucille was in an intimate relationship that had the potential for becoming sexual.

Until Lucille began to tame her gremlin, she was not only good and righteous but was also emotionally isolated and unable to enjoy sexual intimacy.

Baba Rub Adub

Michael's gremlin was ancient. He had long hair and a beard, a white robe, and sat in the lotus position. He frequently reminded Michael of his innate unworthiness and pressed him to seek "higher consciousness" in the name of "spirituality." He made clear to Michael that to have nice things was materialistic and that materialism took him off the path to spirituality, and not to be spiritual was very bad. According to Baba Rub Adub, having only necessities was spiritual, and spiritual was good. In one of our early sessions, Michael let me know in no uncertain terms that he didn't buy into the "more is better" myth. (Except, of course, that more poverty was apparently infinitely superior to less poverty.)

Michael's gremlin had him caught up in the worst kind of materialism: *spiritual materialism.* I think gremlins that inspire this style of living are among the most dastardly, because they misdirect the souls on which they labor from seeking the truth within themselves, instead getting them caught up in the accoutrements of spirituality. *Spiritual materialism* is no different from what we usually think of as *materialism.* Different trappings. Same trap.

The Grim Reaper

Dorothy was 34 when our paths crossed. She was married and the mother of three children. Her lifestyle resembled a modified version of the *Father Knows Best* television series of the '50s. Her living situation looked to others almost exactly as she intended. When I met Dorothy she was spending her time taking her children to school, cleaning house, going to the grocery store, watching television, and suffering almost constant, barely tolerable emotional pain.

20

I have met many people with gremlins
similar to Dorothy's. It is strange but true that
there are vast numbers of people walking around on
the planet who believe that feeling hassled, disgruntled, bummed out, low, and "in a funk" is a natural way
of being. For some people, this is the only style of existence they know. This was the case with Dorothy.

Having problems and worrying were Dorothy's way of
life. In a sense, they were her entertainment. She spent a
great deal of time in a world of make-believe, analyzing situations, fearing the future, and regretting the past. While
she felt far less than terrific, on some level she was comfortable. Worrying kept her occupied and allowed her to
avoid making contact with the real world, for it is impossible to be lost in worry about the future and/or the past
and fully relate to the real world at the same time.

Some of the emotional sufferers I have met even
use suffering as a basis for relationships (not to be
confused with friendships). I have known people

whose relationships with others revolved entirely around their helping one another with whatever hassles are current for them. Dorothy's Grim Reaper gremlin perpetuated the notion that suffering was not only natural but noble. He sometimes taunted her with the promise that suffering in the present would lead her to contentment at a later date. For Dorothy to choose to do something other than suffer emotionally was very difficult.

Like most people who are enmeshed with a Grim Reaper or the like, Dorothy was unaware of her habit of suffering. She was, one might say, "in it." She did not realize her control over how she felt or her ability to choose to enjoy herself and her life. Gremlins who take the form of the Grim Reaper are vicious and tenacious. They can, however, be tamed.

Little Miss What-the-Hell

Katrina is a high-powered, high-profile attorney in her early 50s. She came to me saying she wanted to "get control of her life." The symptom that concerned her most was her overeating—mostly sweets. She explained that for weeks she might be admirably self-disciplined, but (I think probably because she was human) on occasion she would be less than perfect and treat her taste buds to a small sample of something "sugary and gooey." When she did so, however, her gremlin, a rather playful hussy wearing black fishnets and a red dress cut up high as the national debt, would step out of the shadows saying, "Oh, what the hell," at which point the floodgates of self-discipline would come tumbling down, and Katrina would dive headlong into a no-limit dessert orgy.

No sooner had she done so than the very same Little Miss What-the-Hell who had initiated the food frenzy would charge in with this line: "Now you've done it. You'll never change."

This cycle had repeated itself for almost all of Katrina's fifty years—until she began to witness her gremlin. She now has a sense of humor about Little Miss What-the-Hell and claims she has even learned a thing or two from her about lightening up and having a bit of raucous fun once in a while. But Katrina has lost twenty-two pounds in the last three months, eats sweets on occasion, and tells me that her entire experience regarding food and her body is no longer fraught with the anguish she had always known.

GREMLIN MYTHS

From the few gremlins you've now met, you may have noticed that gremlins tend to perpetuate myths about people, life, and the nature of the universe. Often the myths they use to cloud our pure experience have been around for so long and are so much a part of our existence that we are unaware of them.

So that you might become sensitized to some of your own gremlin's myths, I have listed below a few of the most common hypnotic myths used by gremlins I have met:

- **The natural you is unlovable and/or unacceptable.**
- **To show sadness is to be weak, childish, unreliable, or overly dependent.**
- **Suffering is noble.**
- **Fast is good and slow is bad.**
- **Nice girls don't enjoy sex.**
- **Nice girls certainly don't show that they enjoy sex.**

23

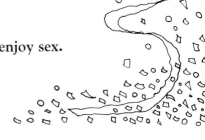

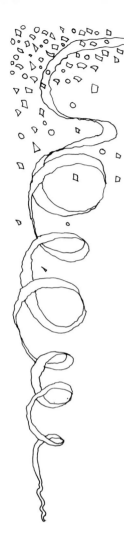

- To show anger is to be out of control, childish, unprofessional, and/or sinful.
- To express uncensored joy is to be silly or unprofessional.
- Not acknowledging and/or not expressing emotions will make them go away.
- Not taking care of unfinished business will make it disappear.
- Men are better leaders than women.
- More is better.
- Less is better.
- Worry has value.
- Anxiety has value.
- Guilt has value.
- Eastern philosophy and religion are truer to the heart than Western philosophy and religion.
- Western philosophy and religion are truer to the heart than Eastern philosophy and religion.
- Someday you will get your ducks in a row.
- Tensing in anticipation of pain lessens its impact.
- _____
- _____
- _____
- _____
- _____

You'll notice I left a few blank spaces above. I did so because I'm certain that as you become more and more astute at simply noticing your very own gremlin, you will become aware of some of the myths he uses to dampen your happiness. Some may be obvious to you already. If so, you might want to jot them down in the spaces provided. I'd also love for you to share them with me. There's a way to do so on the Gremlin Taming Institute™ Web page, which, as you may have guessed, is www.tamingyourgremlin.com.

A FEW WORDS ABOUT THE GREMLIN-TAMING METHOD™

Taming your gremlin® is a simple (not to be confused with easy) process. Taming your gremlin can be an enjoyable process. Taming your gremlin takes practice and persistence. Taming your gremlin requires the sort of effort implied by words like *allowing* and *letting*, not by words like *trying* and *straining*.

There are three basic processes involved in taming your gremlin. These are:

Simply Noticing

Choosing and Playing with Options

Being in Process

3
More About
Simply Noticing

To *simply notice* is to be aware—to pay attention. *Simply noticing* has nothing to do with asking yourself why you are the way you are, although these answers may become obvious to you as you learn to simply notice you being you.

In taming your gremlin, it is important to *simply notice* how you are—not *why* you are how you are, but *how* you are. *Thinking about* and *simply noticing* are very different processes.

Thinking about is a preferred activity of your gremlin. It's a way of keeping you out of touch with the natural you—the observer.

Simply noticing, on the other hand, is what happens when you experience the natural you and your surroundings *without* input from your gremlin.

Thinking about is, of course, a boon and a thrill much of the time. While you are certainly not just your thoughts, you would be a bore without them. But when it comes to Gremlin-Taming, *simply noticing* is more efficient and effective than *thinking about*. *Simply noticing* is the first and most important step in the Gremlin-Taming Method™. Your equipment for *simply noticing* is your awareness.

REALMS OF AWARENESS

Awareness is a tool. At any point you can choose to focus your awareness on any one of three realms:

Your Body

or

The World Around You

or

The World of Mind

When you focus your awareness on *your body* or on the *world around you* via your sensory receptors, you are grounded in the *here* and *now*. When, however, you focus your awareness on your thoughts, fantasies, ideas, and memories, you are involved in the *world of mind*.

In the world of mind you can spend time reliving the past, rehearsing for the future, making meaning out of what you notice about your body or the world around you, or simply entertaining yourself. To dwell in the world of mind is neither good nor bad. It is often productive to learn from the past or to plan for the future. Fantasy can be very entertaining, and certainly it is necessary in order for creativity to occur. To lead a full, rich life, however, and to tame your gremlin and tap into the natural you, it is helpful to be conscious of the flow of your awareness from your body—to the world around you—to the world of mind.

In every moment you are a devotee. In every moment you devote your life to something. You do so via your awareness.

27

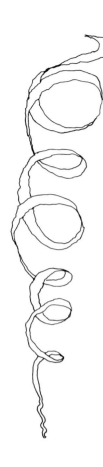

Your awareness is a spotlight mounted in the current moment. From its base in this moment called *now*, you are directing it. You can shine it on these words, on what is going on around you, or on what is going on within you. You can send it into the past via your gift of memory, or you can frighten or enlighten your psyche by imagining the future. You can let your awareness pan aimlessly through the meanderings of your mind and use your mind to analyze, chastise, or aggrandize. You can focus your awareness with the precision of a laser or broaden it, drawing into your experience a range of facts, fantasies, and fantastic goings-on. You can shift your awareness slowly from possibilities to people or let it flit from one aspect of your experience to another. In each moment, consciously or unconsciously, you choose. It's your choice. It's your life. Your awareness can lead you or you can lead it. And that choice is with you *here* and *now*.

In relationship to your spotlight of awareness, you can be a passenger or a driver, a victim or a participant, a pawn or a player. You choose. Not once and for all, but in each moment of your precious life—the life that is shooting through you now and at every other moment of your existence. To maximize the richness of the experience of your very own life is to take charge of your spotlight of awareness right here, right now.

Consciously focusing your awareness requires effort. It does not require strain. Consciously guiding your spotlight of awareness from its base in the *here* and *now* is a gentle process. And it's a pleasure.

Consciously is a key word here. You've been shining that spotlight around for years, and sometimes you've done it consciously. But if you were more conscious and sharpened your attention, imagine the possibilities. Imagine how you would feel.

Taking charge of your spotlight of awareness is about being willing to experience fully your very own existence, including your unique thoughts and emotions and experiences of the world, without the contamination of your gremlin's chatter and without the filter of preconceived notions or other people's ideas. It's about trusting your own senses in the present moment. It's about having the courage to recognize that your life is a time-limited gift given directly to you and treating it as such in every choice you make. It's about honing your own *response ability*. It's about taking care, with your life and with your awareness.

Your gremlin will raise objections to these simple truths. He may be doing so at this very moment. He wants you to feel lousy and less than fully vibrant and alive, so he may fuss, rant, and rave, or hit you with some lengthy, diversionary pontification. Notice his chatter. You may even gain some appreciation for his persistence and creativity. After all, he's been with you since your early years and he's developed his methods based on his thorough knowledge of you and of your unique vulnerabilities. He is determined to hypnotize you into believing life is complex, difficult, and perhaps even painful. And he is a full-time devotee of this purpose. Notice his chatter, but do so without taking his chatter too seriously.

Sometimes, when we're not consciously directing our spotlight of awareness, we slip unknowingly into the *world of mind*, which often is no more than a world of make-believe. If, for example, you and I were talking right now and I saw you looking at me, I might imagine that you were listening to me, that you were bored, that you were angry with me, or any combination of these or who knows what? I might even predicate my actions on my fantasy. If I imagined that you were listening to me, I probably would continue talking. If I imagined you were bored, I might stop talking. If I imagined you were angry with me, I might get uptight and begin communicating with you defensively. My action would be based on fantasy, and my fantasy would, in all likelihood, be based on past experiences rather than on the reality of the current moment.

Taming your gremlin does not involve staying out of the world of mind. It simply involves making certain that you enter the world of mind by choice.

Your awareness will serve you best when you gently focus it. Terms like *spaced out* or *foggy* describe your existence when your awareness is not focused. Being spaced out is no more than generalizing your awareness, that is, taking in too much at once, with no sharp foreground to your experience.

You often have a choice about what you bring into the foreground of your experience and what you relegate to background. Taking charge of your awareness and consciously guiding it from its base in the *here* and *now* is how you exercise that choice. A key word when it comes to focusing your awareness is *slow*. A key phrase is *simply noticing*.

Many people grow up believing that their awareness extends only to those boundaries defined by the limits of their senses. Other people claim to be clairvoyant and to have awareness beyond their physical senses. Whether or not your awareness is expanded beyond your physical senses is totally irrelevant when it comes to taming your gremlin and to fully enjoying yourself and your gift of life. Regardless of how expansive or how limited your senses are, you must still learn to gently focus your awareness if you are to tame your gremlin.

When you practice establishing the *here* and *now* as a home base from which you consciously control your spotlight of awareness, it will be helpful to you to reflect on two fundamental tenets:

Remember where you end and all else begins.
Breathe, dammit, breathe.

REMEMBER WHERE YOU END AND ALL ELSE BEGINS

On some level we are all one. Sounds like ethereal woo-woo, I know, but it's true. It doesn't mean that you're me or that I'm you. It just means that on the deepest level we are all the same pure energy. But—and this is an important "but"—on this physical plane of existence, the one where we go bowling and lose our keys, there is a miraculous sheath separating you from the rest of the world. It is a wonderful sheath. It's incredibly sensitive to the world that surrounds you. It's an amazing organ called—you guessed it—your skin.

Your skin has more nerve endings than any other part of your body. It is waterproof and tough. Even when the top layer gets rubbed off, which it does constantly (you'll shed about thirty disgusting pounds of dead skin in this lifetime), it is replaced by living layers below. You exist within the boundary defined by this relatively thin organ. (It's about two millimeters thick in most places.)

Your skin is a miraculous organ. It is surrounded by an energy field, and it is so sensitive that you can feel certain properties within your environment without actually coming in contact with them. Equally amazing is that while your skin is a sensitive receptor, it is also a boundary, a vibrating boundary that separates you from all else.

From within the boundary defined by your skin you are peering out at these words. Within that boundary you are interpreting them. Within it you are breathing. From within the boundary defined by your skin you get bummed out, wrought up, and turned on. From within the boundary defined by your skin you have every experience you have in this life. Events occur around you, but your experience of those events occurs within the boundary defined by your skin.

In the next few days, experiment with noticing your skin. Just be aware of it as a sensitive receptor and as a boundary within which you exist.

BREATHE, DAMMIT, BREATHE

In chapter I we acknowledged the indefinable, infinite power that is the essence of the natural you, and we labeled it *life*. Whatever we call it, one thing is for sure: when it leaves your body, even your best friends won't want to hang with you for any length of time. That infinite force powers the finite body within which you live and via which you are attending to these words:

> **Your physical body and this life force have come together to form the entity that answers to your name. They are joined by your breath. Breathing is worth noticing and appreciating.**

Eventually you will stop breathing and your body will rot. Until then, gently, without hyperventilating, simply make certain to take in all of the fresh air your body needs and desires, and to exhale fully. How and what you breathe affects your health and your disposition. Proper breathing for healthy people under healthful circumstances comes easily. Millions of happy infants and soundly-sleeping grown-ups do it constantly without effort. As for you, if you take into your lungs too little good, clear oxygen, you are sure to get tense, blue, and probably ill. If you take in too much without exhaling it completely, you will get woozy and act strange.

My first draft of this chapter contained an elaborate description of what happens in your body when you breathe, as well as a specific breathing activity I use with my clients and students. I chucked them both. The explanation took too many words, and breathing is such a fundamental (and important) experience that writing about it felt contrived. Here's what I'd like you to know:

Full, clear breathing is important. It entails liberal and lively movement of your abdomen outward as you inhale and inwardly as you exhale. This sounds backward to some people, and it might to you. Your tendency may be to pull your abdomen in when you inhale and force it out when you exhale. This stomach in/chest out style of inhalation allows you to fill only the upper portion of your lungs. It's the way you breathe when you're having a gremlin attack. It is a breathing style that is common to all of us when we feel threatened or anxious, but folks who breathe this way habitually are often people who are perpetually fearful and suspicious, usually because of hurtful past experiences. They tend to distrust them-selves and others. This type of breathing and the bodily tension that accompanies it are an attempt to brace against life rather than to live in it.

When you cramp your breathing, you block emotions and limit your ability to sense and fully experience the

world around you. Your awareness becomes concentrated in your intellect to the exclusion of your body and sensory receptors. We all do this to some extent at times, such as when we are grappling with some unresolved issue from our past, analyzing a dilemma, or trying too hard to predict or mentally prepare for the future. These cerebral processes are important and have their place in controlled doses. But too much thought can result in you missing life as it is unfolding for you right now, and can make you anxious and fretful. Proper breathing can help you maintain an efficient balance between your use of your intellect and your use of your natural senses. It can help you connect with and begin to trust the natural you—the observer.

When your breathing is relaxed and clear and you are taking in all of the air you want and are exhaling fully, you will be more aware of yourself and more aware of the props and players in your world. You will be more aware of where you end and they begin, more aware of that miraculous sheath known as your skin, and most important, more open to a full experience of the life force within you. In short, your perceptions will be clearer and your vantage point for responding to change will be better.

If clear, full, relaxed breathing has not been your habit, you may find when you try it that you feel uncomfortably vulnerable. We have been socialized into tensing in anticipation of pain, as if this will prevent or lessen the pain that we fear. Bogus information.

To tense against pain is counterproductive. Tensing, in fact, initiates, perpetuates, and prolongs pain. Experiment with staying aware of your skin and keeping your breathing clear. If you notice this leaves you feeling vulnerable, play with thinking of the feeling of vulnerability as a simple state of relaxed attentiveness.

Your breathing can serve you as both a barometer and a regulator of the extent to which you dive into an all-out experience of your life. Notice differences in your breathing as you encounter different kinds of situations, like when greeting someone special to you. Or in a negotiation with someone you distrust. Experimenting with proper breathing in various circumstances, while simple, can be invigorating and, in a way, confronting. When you do choose to experiment with monitoring and regulating your breathing, get into it. Practice.

Practice is important. You can read this book or others until you're a walking, talking, enviable encyclopedia of facts and philosophies on the betterment of humankind, and while you might impress your friends with your library and your vocabulary, none of your knowledge will amount to a hill of beans unless you get serious enough to turn theory into action through *practice*.

A PRACTICE SESSION

Here is an activity to help you learn to gain gentle control over your awareness. I suggest you take a few moments to read the indented section that follows, and when you're in a mood to experiment and can arrange for ten to fifteen minutes of uninterrupted solitude, find a comfortable place to sit, close your eyes, and practice.

Focus your spotlight of awareness on your breathing. Gently concentrate on a few breaths, noticing the movement of the air through your nose, down your trachea, and into your lungs. Pay very close attention to the movement of your abdomen as you breathe, taking care to allow your belly to round out as you inhale and allowing it to collapse inward as you exhale. Make certain to draw into your lungs all the air that you want. There's no need to hyperventilate or to breathe heavily. Simply take in all the air that you want and, when you exhale, exhale fully, blowing out the last bit of air. Breathe at a pace that is comfortable for you.

Your awareness may drift. It may go to your mental processes (the world of mind), to a sound (the world that surrounds you), or to an itch or some other bodily sensation. It is natural for your awareness to wander. However, at the point that you become aware that this is happening, consciously bring your awareness back to your breathing, tracing breaths in and out of your body.

Controlling and guiding your awareness is a very gentle process. It is not something you *try* to do. It is something you *allow* yourself to do. Be gentle with yourself. Do this for a minute or two. Go slowly and relax.

Once you are breathing comfortably, allow your awareness to focus on the surface of your skin.

Your skin is a receptor. It is an organ. And if you will attend to it, you will be able to feel air on your skin, your clothes against your skin, and even perspiration and hair. For one or two minutes, gently guide your awareness back and forth between your breathing and your skin.

Not only is your skin a very sensitive receptor, it is also a boundary. It separates you from all other matter in the universe. While this may seem too obvious to mention, I recommend that for a brief moment, while keeping your breathing clear and noticing your skin, that you attend to your physical separateness from the world around you. Simply attend to your skin as a vibrating boundary between you and the rest of the world. Pay attention to your separateness from all else. Experience yourself as being encased by your skin. Pay special attention to the weight of your eyelids on your eyes, and for a few moments, practice directing your awareness from:

your eyelids,

to

your breathing,

to

the surface of your skin.

Play with gently directing your awareness among these three areas, and when you are ready, with an awareness of your breathing and your skin, inhale slowly, once again, imagining your breath passing behind your heart and brushing gently against it. As you do so, say in your mind the words, "I'm taming."

Then, exhale fully, again feeling your breath pass lightly over the back of your heart. In your mind say the words, "My gremlin."

Notice the surface of your skin once again.

Gently lift your eyelids. It will be as if you are peering out from within your body into a multidimensional movie—*the world around you.* You may at this same instant be aware of your skin tingling and feeling very alive. I call this state of separateness *being centered.*

37

BEING CENTERED

Being centered is simply one way of being. For goodness' sake, do not give yourself some kind of rule in the form of *should* or *ought to* when it comes to being centered. To tell yourself you should be centered or ought to be here now is to set up a duality between your natural self and your gremlin.

Think of being centered as your home base in the *here* and *now*, and go home often. Each time you return home, you are giving yourself a fresh start.

I strongly recommend that you center yourself every day, preferably in the morning. Having established a feeling of centeredness as your home base, you will be able to return to it more easily when you get knocked off center during the day—and you will. With practice, you'll be able to re-center yourself in a few breaths' worth of time by simply focusing briefly on your breathing, and then on the surface of your skin. Use your "I'm taming my gremlin" mantra. Blink slowly, and as you lift your eyelids, you might say something to yourself like:

> **"The world was created five seconds ago complete with props, players, and history."**
>
> or
>
> **"I just arrived on the planet with a head full of ideas and memories to which I can give whatever importance I choose."**

So let's review. Here are some fill-in-the-blank items to which I'll bet you can easily respond.

Your primary skill when it comes to taming your gremlin is to simply n _ t _ _ e. The tool you use to simply notice is your spotlight of a w _ _ _ n _ s s. Your spotlight of awareness is placed on a pedestal in the here and n _ _. To establish the here and _ _ _ as a home base from which you shine your spotlight of a w _ r _ n _ _ s, you will want to pay close attention to your b r _ _ t _ _ n _ and to the miraculous sheath, known as your s _ _ n, that separates you from the rest of the world. When centering yourself, you may make use of your new mantra, "I'm taming my g r _ _ l _ n." As you practice putting this information to use day to day and breath to breath, you will become more centered.

Being c _ n _ _ r _ d and establishing the *here* and *now* as a home base from which you shine your spotlight of awareness is a powerful tool when it comes to Gremlin-Taming.

When it comes to having a truly satisfying existence, a basic tenet of operation, and one that people often look right past, is:

Feeling good is primarily an inside job.

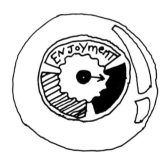

AN INSIDE JOB

The world is filled with props and players. There are millions of props and players in your world, and they interrelate with one another and with you to form circumstances—some good, some bad, some horrific. Each set of circumstances represents an opportunity to practice centering.

Centering and re-centering is the key to a successful reckoning with the whips and scorns of time.

If your eyes are following these words, you've been around the block enough times to know that when it comes to maximizing pleasure and minimizing pain, often it's simply handier to be skilled at regulating your level of cool, calm, collected contentment regardless of circumstances than for your happiness to be dependent on trying to change them.

Your gremlin would have you believe that you will be content and satisfied when you get your ducks in a row, never telling you that your idea of a straight line may not remotely resemble what the universe has in mind. And God only knows what the universe has in mind.

It's swell to have goals. Achieving them can enhance your pleasure, but on this "ducks in a row" thing, how about a reality check? Even if you get the little dickens to line up in a neat, dutiful row for a spell, they won't stay that way for any length of time. When it comes to "once and for all,"

you will never get your ducks in a row.

Look around you. As a full-fledged participant observer in this game of life, you must have noticed that where your circumstances are concerned, if all is going badly, it will get better. And if all is going along quite well, it will take a turn for the worse. Such is human existence. It's so. You and I can stamp our feet and complain about it, but it's so. And given it's so, doesn't it make sense to put at least as much effort into mastering your inner ability to maintain and restore your balance as you put into controlling your external circumstances? Are you really willing to sample contentment and satisfaction only on those rare occasions when the props and players in your life form themselves into configurations that please you? Centering and the ability to restore your balance swiftly are important skills to have. So here's another method for doing so.

NOW I AM AWARE

Another method of centering yourself is to play a simple game called "Now I Am Aware." Going slowly, simply focus your awareness on one aspect after another of your *here* and *now* experience. Take the time to really notice whatever you bring into your field of awareness, be it a sound, a sight, a smell, something you touch, or something you taste. Go slowly. As you gain relaxed control of your spotlight of awareness, experiment with relocating it from your body—to the world around you—to the world of mind, staying a few seconds in each place. As thoughts come into your awareness, simply notice them and let them go. Gently direct your awareness back inside the boundary defined by your skin, or outside of it, beginning phrases with "Now I am aware of . . ."

41

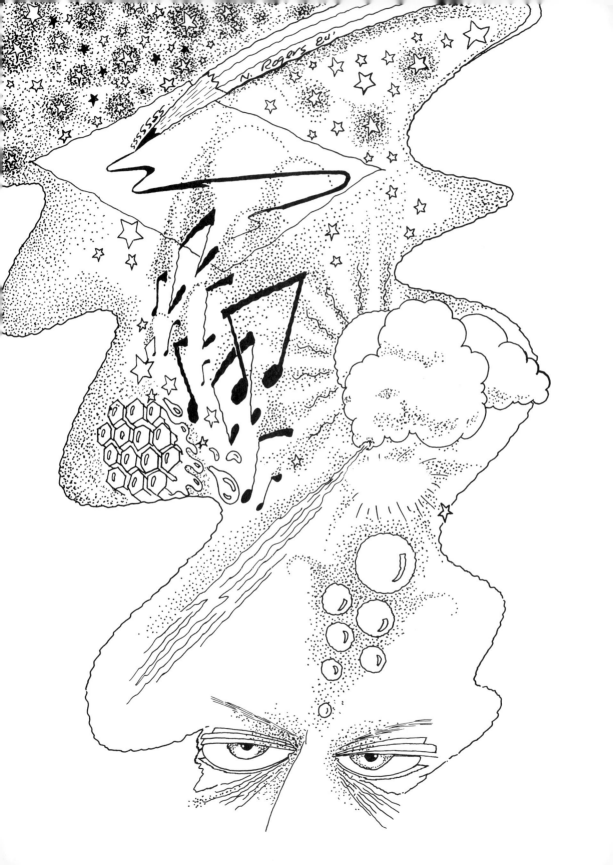

As for me:

"Now I am aware of the sound of the pencil lead
on the paper;
Now I hear music in the background;
Now I am aware of the breeze on my skin;
Now I am aware of thinking about what to write;
Now I am aware of a tightness around my eyes."

Your gremlin will want you to spend no time at all going slowly and increasing your awareness. He knows the power of *simply noticing* as a tool for taming him, and it frightens him. He will do his best to distract you. His monologue, should you detect it, might sound like scolding, or disoriented jabber, like advice from a true friend, or even like interesting intellectual pontification. In any event, it is your gremlin. Simply notice him without allowing yourself to become involved with him. If you find yourself engaged with him, simply channel your awareness back to your body or the world around you, using the words, "Now I am aware."

SIMPLY NOTICING YOUR GREMLIN

Until now, observing your gremlin may have been difficult, perhaps because of the enmeshed quality of your relationship with him. However, as you increase your ability to center yourself in the *here* and *now* and to control your awareness, you will begin to experience more detachment from your gremlin. From a position of being centered, you will become more aware of him. You can feel him, and though your experience of your gremlin may be subtle at first, it is undeniable. You might notice tightness in your chest, a queasy feeling or knot in your stomach, a tension in your shoulders, neck, or back, or an unexplained anxiousness. As you begin to *simply notice* him or her, you will begin to get a sliver of light between the natural you and your gremlin.

In these moments, you are no longer enmeshed with your gremlin. You are his observer. Notice the simple pleasure of this experience. While hardly noticeable in the beginning, the experience is deeply powerful. *Simply notice* it and *simply notice* your gremlin. Don't fret or strain to get a sense of what I'm describing lest you form an expectation of yourself. Your gremlin would love nothing better. Then he can taunt you for being an ineffectual and unsuccessful amateur. Just relax, *simply notice*, and get what you get. As you shine your spotlight on that monster of the mind, while you may not detect his voice, you will likely be able to experience it and him and to get at least a slight feel for his speed, his intensity, and his effect on your body.

If you relax, you may even experience certain colors that seem to go with your gremlin. You may experience his size or his shape. Again, becoming aware of your gremlin is not something that requires intellectual knowledge, strain, study, or even intense concentration. It involves only relaxing and *simply noticing*. It is something you allow yourself to do, not something you try to do.

44

If you begin to have a clear experience, image, or fantasy of your gremlin, you might want to jot down some words that describe him. You might even want to sketch a picture of him. Chances are, by the time you finish this book, you will have more than one picture. Remember, gremlins regularly change their style of being. Yours may have a very distinct look on occasion, and at other times be rather vague. He may be large or small, human or inhuman, colorful or bland, distinct or amorphous. From your vantage point of being centered, your ability to detect his presence will increase.

As you observe him, you will become aware of some of the tactics he uses to stifle your enjoyment. We are about to spend some time refining our abilities to *simply notice* these. Our primary tool will be *awareness*. Remember that the Gremlin-Taming Method involves three essential processes:

Simply Noticing

Choosing and Playing with Options

Being in Process

4

Simply Notice
Your Habits

Your gremlin has trapped you into forming habits for living your life. These habits, or habitual behavior patterns, fall into two general categories:

Habits for Responding to Emotions

Habits for Responding to People and Circumstances

YOUR HABITS FOR RESPONDING
TO EMOTIONS

Emotions fall into five basic categories: anger, joy, sadness, sexual feeling, and fear. When one of these emotions is conjured up, your response may be a habitual one based on a belief rooted in the past. For example, if you learned from experience or from being told that anger is hurtful and that its expression is mean, dangerous, or simply uncouth, your habit may be to block your anger. The same may be true if you equate joy with immaturity, sadness with weakness, sex with promiscuity, or fear with cowardice.

It is difficult to become aware of your habitual behavior patterns because, to borrow an old adage, you can't see the forest for the trees. It is as if you are *of* your habits—until, that is, you begin to *simply notice* them. As you begin to practice being centered, to establish the *here* and *now* as a home base and to regulate the flow of your *awareness* from your body, to the world around you, to the world of mind, your habitual behavior patterns will become more and more obvious to you.

Anger

You may notice, for example, that your habitual physical response to anger is to shorten your breathing. Your habit may be to talk yourself out of your anger, to rationalize it, to rant and rave, to eat, to drink, to fight, or to depress yourself by unconsciously suppressing it. You may experience anger as powerful, as scary, as sexy, or as disgusting. You might become energized, nauseous, vengeful, super-nice, sarcastic, placating, attacking, or very analytical, or you might go to outrageous lengths to avoid the feeling.

I suggest that beginning today you pay close attention to your habitual responses to your experience of anger, keeping in mind that your anger may, at times, take the form of a minor irritation, while at other times you may experience it as a tidal wave of rage. It is unnecessary to analyze your feeling however you experience it. Simply notice the effect of anger on your body, especially on your breathing. When you choose not to express it, what do you do with it instead? You may find that you store it in your stomach, your neck, your shoulders, your head, or your back. I'm certainly not suggesting that you should always express your anger. I am suggesting only that you *simply notice* your habits for responding to this emotion. Are you more comfortable expressing anger with men, women, young people, or old people? What happens to your voice when you get angry? *Simply notice.*

The following experiment will help you get a handle on

47

some of your beliefs about the nature of anger. It is on these beliefs that your habitual behavior patterns regarding anger are based. Center yourself; then read the following items in a state of relaxed concentration and allow yourself to fill in the blanks with your honest reactions.

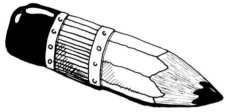

1. I imagine that those who know me well would say that when I am angry I _____

_____.

2. When I'm angry with someone I know well, I tend to _____

_____.

3. When I'm angry with someone I don't know well, I tend to _____

_____.

4. If I suspect someone is angry with me, I feel

_____

and I tend to _____.

5. A recent time I felt angry at another person was

_____

_____.

6. At that time, I chose to _____

_____ _____.

7. As I remember that experience now, I notice
that I _____

_____.

8. If I had allowed my anger to be reflected in my
voice and my words in a manner that was
absolutely uncensored, I imagine that I would
have _____

_____.

9. Then I think I would have felt _____

_____.

10. When my mother was angry, she tended to

_____

_____.

11. When my father was angry, he tended to

_____

_____.

Look over your responses to the statements above.
They offer clues to your habits regarding anger. There is
no need for you to be cautious about acknowledging your
beliefs and/or habits. Doing so does not imply that you

need to change anything. Of course, your gremlin will have you judge your responses. Instead, *simply notice* and relax. However you responded to these items is fine, and remember: even if you spot a pattern for handling your anger that you aren't proud of, you don't have to change it. If you want to play with an option, that's fine. We'll talk in depth about playing with options later, but for now, let go of any judgment and *simply notice.*

If you become aware of beliefs or habits relevant to your reaction to anger, you may wish to jot them down. Think through the validity of these beliefs or habits for you at this stage of your life, remembering that a habit that made sense when it was formed may have little value in your life *here* and *now.* You might want to make a different choice. Or not.

Now, what about sadness, sexual feeling, fear, and joy? Yes, joy.

Joy

I meet people frequently who suppress joy. I love the late Charles Schulz's pictures of Snoopy doing his suppertime dance. Such open joy is a beautiful thing. But some folks confuse explosive joy with irresponsibility, immaturity, and being out of control (sometimes as a result of the "children should be seen and not heard" belief). Such notions are the tools of your gremlin.

A full expression of delight is not only good for the health and disposition of the bearer, it powerfully affects even those around you.

I remember a day in 1983 when I took my son, Jonah, to Stubbs Barbecue in Lubbock, Texas, for lunch. Jonah was 6 at the time. While he gnawed on the ribs of some blessed bovine, I nibbled carrot sticks and jalapeños and chowed down on a baked potato the size of a cantaloupe. I'd been a strict vegetarian for five years. I ate no meat, red or otherwise, no eggs or animal products, and no fish. After picking the last rib clean, Jonah leaned back in his chair and took a drink of Coke. Then he licked his lips and the tips of all ten of his beautiful little metacarpals and flashed me as big and as joyful a grin as I've ever seen. I lost it. I leapt out of my chair, ran up to the counter, and ordered a chopped beef sandwich and a beer. The floodgates came crashing down, and I'm just as close to God and what's right as ever—I think.

My point, of course, is not "eat more meat." It is simply that authentic, uncensored joy is powerful, beautiful, and contagious. What is more, the experience of joy is always available right inside your very own body. As you begin to get more and more space between you and your gremlin you will feel it more often, for sure.

And as for sadness, did you know that a full experience of sadness can feel invigorating?

Sadness

Many people confuse sadness with depression. Actually, sadness and depression are very different experiences. Sadness is a natural response to certain stimuli. It often results in tears and full breathing. It can be a powerful, rich, enlivening experience. Depression, on the other hand, is often the result of blocking sadness, or of blocking anger. Depression is what can happen when our gremlin convinces us that our feelings are unacceptable. When we are depressed, we have a sense of being deadened and blocked. When we fully experience our sadness, we may not feel on top of the world, but we will feel very much alive and may even have a sense of well-being. Most importantly, when we experience our emotions fully, we will eventually move through them to a new feeling space. On the other hand, if we avoid our emotions, we tend to stay stuck in a particular emotional state.

What do you habitually do with your sadness?

Recall a time when you felt sad, over a loss, perhaps, or in a sad movie. How did you react? Did your gremlin convince you to legislate against your sadness? If so, you probably started breathing rather shallowly and developed a tight, full feeling in your throat, or a headache. That was your choice, and in some instances it may be better to suffer these physical sensations than to cry. To start sobbing at a time when the repercussions would cause you pain or embarrassment wouldn't do much to help you to enjoy your life, now would it? Remember, the key here is to operate out of choice, rather than out of habit. What you do with your sadness is for you to decide; not once and for all, but on each occasion in which your sadness emerges. There is, however, value in observing your habits for responding to anger, joy, and sadness, because operating out of habit is what your gremlin uses to lead you into a state of misery.

Anger and sadness emerge in a variety of situations. Often they accompany the experience of loss. You can lose your wallet, the big game, or a loved one. It's sandpaper-rough when it's the last one.

A loving soul is a loving soul, whether it's housed in a predominantly hairless body with two arms and two legs, or in one with four legs and fur. If you've had a loving relationship with another soul and that soul makes his or her leap to the other side, you'll have some healing to do. If someone you love dies, mourn. Don't be shy about crying or reticent to sing his or her praises. Actively warm yourself

52

with good memories, cringe at bad ones, and curse at regrets. Strong emotions after a loss are natural. Give yourself the time and space to experience them fully. Express your feelings verbally and in writing. Review the past, but don't try to redo it. Do so with a clear intention to heal yourself. This may take days or weeks.

The true love that is the essence of the *natural you* will heal your pain if you allow it to do so, but it requires spending time with your emotions—feeling them, experiencing them. Trust the process and eventually you will arrive at a point of choice regarding your behaviors when your emotions surface. In some circumstances you may choose to dive into them. At other times you may choose to *simply notice* them, take a breath or two, and gently and respectfully lay them aside for the time being. Notice the experience of choice and of choosing. Then, with conscious self-respect, self-love, and a clear intention to feel good, experiment with reducing time spent in mourning and increasing time spent enjoying the *here* and *now* and in creating a fulfilling future for yourself and the living loves of your life.

Dive into your memories and your pain when you feel the need. Accept unexpected waves of sadness and anger and work with them, not against them. Breathe. Reflect on the gifts you received from having spent time with your lost loved one. Decide to cherish the gifts, to use them, and to embellish them. Forgive your loved one for dying. This, too, takes time. Intend to forgive if you can't yet forgive. Find the desire to let go of your loved one. Let go of him or her. Keep the good memories and wisdom you gained from your loved one's life and death.

Sexual Feeling

Just as your gremlin may convince you or scare you into suppressing your anger, joy, and sadness, he may also put a lid on your sexual feelings. Notice what you tend to do when you feel amorous and/or sexually aroused. Sure, it depends on the circumstances, but has your gremlin convinced you to respond to sexual feelings out of habit?

I've met men whose gremlins had them convinced that ejaculation was a necessary response to feeling turned on. And I have met men and women whose gremlins had convinced them that sexual feeling was unwholesome. Remember Katherine and her gremlin, the Reverend Al Drydup? The Reverend had confused and thwarted Katherine with these two messages: "Sex is nasty and sinful" and "You should save it for the one you love." Confusing, huh? Gremlins are treacherous, tricky, and determined.

Notice your habitual responses to sexual feeling. Do your habits vary from circumstance to circumstance? What does feeling sexually attracted to someone feel like to you? Do you feel weak, strong, wet, warm, angry, anxious, electrified, loving? What happens to your voice? Your level of muscle tension? *Simply notice* over the next few weeks. Just relax and observe. Whatever you notice is fine. You need not judge (your gremlin will do plenty of that). Relax and pay attention.

Fear

Fear can be an enormously powerful experience, but fear is nothing to be afraid of. The physical experience of fear is an important signal—either that there is present or imminent danger, or that you are in the world of mind imagining that there is. If you notice a bull charging headlong in your direction, fear will likely direct you to get yourself out of the pasture. Yet the physical sensation of fear is no less real even if it is not so clearly well-founded: your breathing shortens and quickens, your pulse rate rises, your heart pounds harder, and adrenaline floods your system. Whether your fear is engendered by real-life circumstances or a gremlin attack, it's important to notice your fear, to bring it into the light, and to experience it, if only briefly. The line between fear and excitement is a thin one. More than one professional entertainer has told me that embracing "stage fright" transforms it into excitement, which actually energizes their performance.

There's fear and then there's *fear*. Few faced with the magnitude of an event such as the collapsing World Trade Center towers on September 11, 2001, have the presence of mind to practice the exercise that follows.

But when you are plagued by less horrific fears and you have the time and presence of mind to do so, these four simple questions can help. The questions are: What's so? So what? So what? What now? The rather unremarkable example below arose with one of my clients quite recently.

What's so? (Separate what you know with absolute certainty from what you imagine.)

I saw my supervisor looking in my direction with a frown on her face. I'm imagining she's upset with me and is going to give me a bad review.

So what? (Notice your catastrophic expectation.)

She may fire me.

So what? (If your catastrophic expectation comes true, what's the worst that will happen? Get to your bottom-line fear, which will always have something to do with severe pain, abandonment, or death.)

My life will fall apart. I'll lose everything. My family and I will starve.

What now? (The options are infinite.)

Might as well shoot myself.

I think I'll quit before they fire me.

I'll check out my assumption with my supervisor and ask how she's feeling about me and my job performance.

I'm going to make damn sure I perform my job well.

Throughout this book I've included several interactive exercises that will help you get a handle on some of your ideas and habits regarding your emotions, and on some of your gremlin's wily ways. Everybody has a gremlin to tame, but the particular activity that follows isn't everyone's cup of tea. If you decide to give it a go, do so at a time when you are willing to dive into the experience wholeheartedly. You'll get a great deal out of it. If you would rather do the activity later, or not at all, that is just fine—and you will still learn to tame your gremlin.

THE EXPERIENTIAL ACTIVITY THAT ISN'T EVERYONE'S CUP OF TEA

I've guided thousands of people through the following experiential activity (and many more). I can say unabashedly that most participants have benefited tremendously. But I was always there guiding them when they did the activity (usually in a private session or a workshop). Or they were hearing my voice via one of my audio programs. *Here* and *now*, with you and me, it's more challenging because our primary tool of communication is the written word. But I've been experimenting with lots of my trainees and clients, and I know now, beyond a doubt, that if you and I work together, you can have the same sort of deep awareness that occurs in my workshops. Here's your part:

1. Allow yourself fifteen to twenty minutes of uninterrupted solitude in a quiet, comfortable place.
2. Center yourself before beginning, using your "I'm taming my gremlin" mantra on the final breath before opening your eyes.
3. Follow my written instructions precisely.
4. Do not skip ahead.

When you are ready, with this book open to this page and a paper and pen within reach, close your eyes and center yourself. After saying your Gremlin-Taming mantra, open your eyes and begin reading the following text.

In a moment, I'm going to ask you to close your eyes again, and when you do so, to take your spotlight of awareness into the world of mind. Once in the world of mind, you will bring into your awareness an image of a living human. A person you love wholeheartedly—a child, perhaps, or your spouse, or a friend. You genuinely love this person. You may or may not be liking them at the moment, but you've no doubt about your love for them.

In a moment, when you close your eyes, see this person alone and standing. In this fantasy they will not be able to see you, but you will see them quite

57

clearly. Really look at them. Look closely, breathing fully as you do so. Pay special attention to this person's eyes and to the area surrounding their eyes. Periodically redirect your awareness to your breathing and then back to the person's face. Look at them with the same sort of relaxed attentiveness with which you would enjoy a beautiful vista or a work of art. Do so for as long as you would like. Keep your breathing slow, relaxed, and full. *Simply notice your inner experience throughout this activity.* Whatever you experience is fine. There is no way to do this wrong. Rejoin me at the beginning of the next paragraph when you feel finished. Close your eyes and begin now.

Welcome back. Keep your breathing full and clear as you pick up your pen and redirect your spotlight of awareness back here to my words. Let the natural you respond to the statements that follow. Read each statement and express yourself in an open-souled, uncensored manner, with no consideration regarding outcome or your loved one's response. This is not a rehearsal for reality; it is a learning experience just for you. Whatever you write is right.

There is no way to do this wrong.
Keep your breathing clear and full.
Go slowly.

_____, when I entered my imagination
(your loved one's name)
and saw you, I noticed that my breathing was _____

_____ and I felt _____.

As I took the time to really look at you, I noticed that

the area around my heart felt _____, and

my breathing _____.

One thing I noticed about you was that you _____

_____.

You looked _____.

At this moment I feel _____.

Read the following text; then close your eyes and do as instructed.

Go back into your imagination and again call up the image of the person you have been visualizing. In your mind's eye, notice and then vividly describe to your loved one the physical experience of feeling love for them. Do so slowly.

Then, with your eyes still closed, inhale and exhale slowly and then imagine this person saying your name. He or she may, in real life, call you by one or more names or endearments. Imagine your loved one saying them all. You may or may not hear his or her actual voice, but you will be able to feel the resonance of it. Notice your experience as you imagine them speaking your name. Pay special attention to your breathing and the area surrounding your heart. Rejoin me whenever you like. Close your eyes and begin now.

Welcome back. Complete the statements below. Take no more than two breaths' worth of time before responding to each item. No need to overthink.

_____, when you said my name, I felt

(your loved one's name)

_____. I found myself _____

_____.

When I think of you and how much I love and appreciate you, some of the words that come to mind

are: _____

_____

Because I love you, I wish you would _____

_____. If I could have my way, you would

_____.

After reading the following text, reenter the world of mind and connect once again with the image of your loved one.

When you go back into the world of mind, imagine your loved one responding to you from deep within themselves, a place deeper than their persona, a place richer and truer than any agreements, overt or covert, you and they have about who you are to one another. Just imagine it. Make it up. Imagine your loved one being completely open with you as he or she describes to you their thoughts and feelings about you.

Perhaps you're thinking, "But, Rick, I don't know what they would say." Or "he/she/we would never talk this openly."

That's okay. It's just a fantasy and it's just for you. Stretch your imagination. Relax and see what comes. Return here when you are ready. Close your eyes and begin now.

Hello again. Now respond to the following.

_____, when you were about to tell me
  (your loved one's name)

your thoughts and feelings about me, I felt _____

_____ and I wanted to

_____.

_____, I'm aware that I really want
  (your loved one's name)

you to know that _____.

With regard to our relationship, I want to _____

_____ and I want you to _____

_____.

I imagine that if I told you everything I've noticed and written in this exercise, you would _____

_____.

If I described to you face to face how much I love you, I imagine you would _____.

_____, I've just imagined you will
  (your loved one's name)

_____

if I express to you my love.

The advantage in holding on to my imagined idea about how you will react if I express my love to you is

that you, _____, will _____
(your loved one's name)

_____, and I will _____

_____.

If I take the risk to be uncensored with you, then you
might _____.
And then I would feel _____

_____.

I haven't the foggiest notion whether you'll get a hug, a slap, or a blank stare if you actually express yourself this way to someone you love, but one thing is for sure: your gremlin would like nothing better than for you to opt for the status quo. Remember, he loves preconceived notions and hard-and-fast concepts because they ensure boredom, the blahs, the blues, sadness, and emptiness, and result in relationships entering the Dead Zone.

This sort of experiment in free, pure expression of self, even in fantasy, is sure to arouse your gremlin. He'll raise his ugly head because, as you've learned, his primary means of attack is to scare you into leading life in total conformity with preconceived ideas about who you are and how the world works. He'll claim it's in the name of your safety and your best interest. Why, even entertaining the possibility of making a wild-eyed, unabashed run at living the truth of who you are upsets him. He knows that bringing your fears into the light allows the natural you to reevaluate them "in light" of who you are today—not who you were way back when he convinced you to cement those fears in place. So if he pops up, *simply notice* him. For now, that is all, and that is plenty. You needn't try to change a thing.

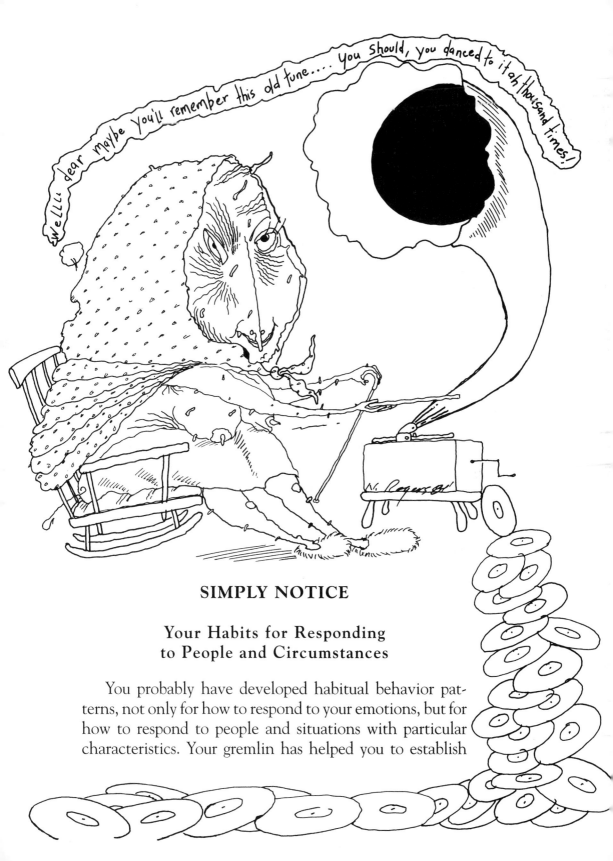

SIMPLY NOTICE

Your Habits for Responding
to People and Circumstances

You probably have developed habitual behavior patterns, not only for how to respond to your emotions, but for how to respond to people and situations with particular characteristics. Your gremlin has helped you to establish these habits and wants you to lead your life in accordance with them. You may be bound and determined not to be judgmental, and the idea of stereotyping people may be repugnant to your nature. Unfortunately, your gremlin loves the idea. He knows that clouding your actual experience with preconceived notions will keep you from experiencing the vibrancy of the current moment.

Your gremlin may have you behaving in the same general way whenever you encounter authority figures, or people with gray hair, or on first dates, or when you are meeting someone for the first time, or when you are in conflict with someone.

You might tend to repeat the same general behaviors over and over in like situation after like situation. These habits are neither good nor bad. However, they may be based on the world as you perceived it at some other time.

Habits that you learned long ago may still be suitable and effective. But they may also be antiquated and limit your enjoyment of your existence. After all, the world for you as an adult is far different from the world you experienced as a child, or even a few years ago. What worked for you in the past may not work as well for you now.

As long as you operate out of habit, you will limit your ability to fully experience, appreciate, and enjoy your gift of life.

By acting out of habit, you will replay the same life dramas over and over again. The characters and settings may vary, but the outcomes generally will be the same.

Life may be one damn thing after another, but it does not have to be the same damn thing over and over again.

Your gremlin will sometimes very subtly convince you that operating out of habit is for your own safety. Notice, however, that if you opt for your habitual behavior patterns time after time, you will begin to feel bored, discontented, possibly depressed, and eventually empty. Empty is what your gremlin wants most for you. Once there, your gremlin has you at the threshold of your demise.

Take this ol' familiar road...

WARNING

DETOUR

Fear As a Gremlin Tool

Habits are cemented in place by fear. Fear is your gremlin's primary tool. At the time he talked you into forming a particular behavior into a habit, that behavior may have made very good sense. If your parents punished you when you expressed anger or discontent as a child, it would have made sense for you to develop a happy-face façade. (This is one of my least favorite façades. People who feel an inner contentment don't have the need to smile all the time.) A behavior that you incorporated as a child will be appropriate in certain situations. To the extent that that behavior is a habit, however, it may interfere with your excitement, your spontaneity, and your potential for creative living. The quality of your life might well be dramatically affected.

Gremlins I have met have created very personalized, fear-inducing, catastrophic threats to terrorize and taunt the souls on which they labor. Some of the lines used by gremlins I've known have included:

If you risk changing, you will . . .

lose friends.

fail.

be wrong.

be poor.

be rejected.

be embarrassed.

and many, many more. Scrutinized closely, these fears are honey-coated derivatives of a very, very ominous and powerful gremlin myth:

If you do not do things your gremlin's way, you will end up alone and/or in severe physical or emotional pain and/or dead.

Your gremlin is not the cute little character he may at first appear to be. He's not fooling around. Remember the good news, however. You can render him entirely impotent as you practice the Gremlin-Taming Method:

Simply Notice
Choose and Play with Options
Be in Process

I hope that you will not give yourself the rule that you *should* change old habits. A new rule is no more than a new habit. Adopt a spirit of adventure. Experiment with change once in a while if you want, but more importantly, *simply notice* your habitual behavior patterns for responding to your emotions, people, and circumstances. These habits are based on *concepts*.

5

Simply Notice
Your Concepts

YOUR SELF-CONCEPT

Your self-concept is faulty and self-limiting for one simple reason: you are more than a concept.

I meet people frequently who are unhappy because they are not living up to their concept of who they are or who they imagine they are supposed to be. Some judge themselves as too passive, others as too sad, others as too greedy, and on and on. I even meet people who are so unhappy with who they think they are that they try to do away with themselves. Sometimes they try this physically, and other times they do it by creating new concepts of how and who they want to be. I've met people who try to fit themselves into one self-concept after another. This is a surefire way to become dissatisfied. Breaking through concepts is a very powerful tool when it comes to Gremlin-Taming.

In my work with families, I have noticed that personal growth and enjoyment begin emerging rapidly once family members begin to recognize that their style of being together does not have to approximate the style of any other family. At the point when family members begin to see clearly the rigidity of their concepts and expectations regarding themselves, one another, and their family as a unit, the pleasure begins. They are then free to go around tapping their creativity and focusing on the goal of developing a dynamic, harmonious mini-society suited to their particular desires and personalities. The same is true for individuals.

When a person becomes excited about who she actually is rather than who she wants to convince herself she is, deep inner satisfaction is close at hand.

True satisfaction and contentment have more to do with actualizing yourself than with actualizing your concept of who you imagine you are supposed to be.

That is to say, true contentment is not the same as *getting your act together*. Feeling good is a product of becoming aware of who you are beneath your act or acts.

Acts

We are all, to some extent, actors. We act in order to get what we want and need from the world. Our acts are often a result of the fears our gremlin has instilled in us. Our acts are very personal in that they incorporate our habits and concepts in all their complexity. As you become aware of the personal acts you have created, you will become aware also that you have created an imaginary audience.

In your audience, sitting front row center, will be your most powerful critic—your gremlin. He may represent a composite of the value judgments made by other people in your imaginary audience. Your audience may include your mother, father, employer, friends, enemies, colleagues, or someone with whom you feel or felt competitive. In short—

your audience is comprised of those whom you allow to have influence over your actions and feelings. At times you will receive critics' acclaim and audience applause. As a result, you will feel very good. At other times the response of your critics will leave you discouraged. Even if you become a very fine actor, if you are inordinately attached to your act, you will notice that you feel empty much of the time, for you will realize that the critics' acclaim and the loud applause from your audience are offered in response to your act rather than to the natural you.

You may have created a façade that is very well liked. You may have one or more very good acts that are even loved. But what of the real you that is inside and behind the act? Are you ever seen, heard, or touched? Because a good act may get you what you want for awhile: the critics' acclaim I mentioned earlier, high self-esteem, a few strokes, or monetary reward, I have devoted part of this chapter to

"The Pleasant Person Act." However, let me simply remind you that you are *not* your act, and that shifting from one act to another does not imply qualitative personal growth or increased comfort with yourself. You may fool a few people, or even most people, but you won't fool yourself.

You Are Not Your Act

Among the acts I have seen in recent years are: Super Executive, Back to the Land Woodsman, Red Hot Mama (or Papa), Urban Cowboy, Pious Puritan, Hard Rocker, Music Groupie, Personal Growth Groupie, Damsel in Distress, Macho Man, and Sensitive Male.

Think of three people you'd really like to think well of you. Pick someone who knows you quite well, such as a family member; someone whom you know only slightly but whom you respect and whose respect you'd like to have; and someone with whom your level of familiarity falls somewhere between the other two. Jot their names down. Imagine these three people having a conversation about you when you are not present—a conversation in which they're telling the absolute truth with regard to their experience of you. It's a no-holds-barred conversation about what they think and feel about you. They are getting down to it. What do you imagine would be said? Gently relax and reflect on this, writing down key words and phrases.

Now ask yourself: What would you *like*
these people to think, feel, and say about you
in a candid conversation? You might learn
something about your act by jotting down
your responses.

Now rate your acting. On a scale of 1 to 10 (with 10
being top of the heap) how do you think you're doing
with each of the above people? Anything you'd like to
change in the way you relate to each of them? If so,
what? Don't be embarrassed. There is nothing wrong
with a good act. Remember, you developed your act(s)
for perfectly logical reasons: to get you what you wanted
and what you believed you needed. Your act may work

superbly or it may be dismally ineffective. The
important undertaking for you is to become
aware that an act is just an act and not to confuse
it with the natural you.

**The soul cannot rest so long as
the identity denies it.**

Some of my clients have even named their more famil-
iar acts. In recent months I've met Lash Larue, the Red
Queen; Clark Kent, the Mild-Mannered Reporter; Sister
Mary Perfect; Peace Love Dove Sigh Blissed-Out Earth

75

Mother; Muscles; Mr. Successful; Laid Back Brother; and many others. Acting can be fun. There's nothing wrong with developing an act. However, to let your gremlin delude you into thinking you are or should be your act will result in your feeling anxious and empty during the times when you perform your act poorly. The hard truth is that your act is just as transparent as everyone else's.

Sooner or later you will disappoint your gremlin and those whose applause you seek. When you do, if you're too attached to your act, it will smart, to put it mildly, and your gremlin will have a heyday. You will not enjoy yourself—and given that your life is a gift, it would be a shame not to enjoy it.

Acts and Relationships

The Big Dogs in my high school had flattops, low foreheads, big necks, and were varsity football players. I had wavy hair, a high forehead, a big neck, and made the varsity football team by the skin of my teeth. But my neck didn't get big from something like farmwork or genetics. It got that way because I ordered a neck strap and barbells from Joe Weider Products and worked out like a madman in an attempt to flee my semi-endomorphic natural state and join the ranks of the Big Dogs, so that, like them, I could strut through the halls with an adoring frosty-haired pompom girl on my arm, or better yet, fate willing, hold her warm and tender body next to mine. By my junior year I had developed a fair to middlin' Big Dog disguise, dating, among others, Sally, our head cheerleader.

The first time I laid eyes on Sally was in a pep rally. She leapt in the air, and as she did so I glimpsed her bright red cheerleader panties. In that moment, a lightning bolt shot directly from Sally's panties into my eye sockets and down into my crotch with such force I had to untuck my shirttail or appear obvious. I fell head over heels for Sally. She became the focus of my existence. I lived to watch Sally walk, touch her, kiss her, smell her perfume, and stick my lively tongue in her dainty little ear. Then, after our third date, I experienced a new set of feelings. I started to *like* Sally. Really like her. I even liked her wit and the wisdom with which she spoke. I'd liked girls before, but this much like and lust all at once shook me up. I liked everything about Sally, a response for which I was totally unprepared. It threw me. I knew well enough how to kiss a girl's lips, hold her hand, and stroke her hair; in other words, I knew what to do with a girl's parts. But I hadn't the foggiest notion what to do with a whole girl—so mostly, when I was with Sally, I just flexed my neck.

Sally consumed my every thought for about six months. I consumed Sally's every thought for about six weeks. I remember the day Sally's feelings seemed to shift.

Sally was on her front porch and I was about ten feet away on a walkway that led from her porch to the curb where my pink and white 1955 Ford was parked. It was lowered in front, pinstriped, and had a spider painted on the dashboard. It must have been a warm day because Sally was wearing shorts and I remember ogling her lovely, oh-so-strokeable, creamy-smooth just-right thighs, the thought of which made me even warmer.

There I stood, drinking in Sally with my eyes, testosterone running rampant. I tried to look cool as a cucumber while flexing my neck. I flexed it hard. It wasn't a first-class coil of muscle, but it wasn't small, either. Though it may have looked small compared to my biceps; I could make my left bicep look like a Christmas

ham by propping it up on the driver's side window ledge of my Ford. I know because I used to drive past store windows to check it out.

I stood facing Sally with my thumbs hung in the front pockets of my Levi's and my shoulders hunched forward in an attempt to give maximum expansion to my neck and look happy-go-lucky at the same time. My feet were parallel and placed a little wider than shoulder-length apart. Great stance. Great act. Then, whammo! From out of nowhere, she zapped me. A straight shot to my bravura. Sally looked at me, puzzled, and asked, "Why are you standing like that?"

My breathing stopped. How'd she know I was standing "like that"? Was I that transparent? I thought I looked loose as a goose, muscular, cool, and kind of tough. Could she tell I was faking it? Could she tell I was flexing my neck to the point of impending paralysis?

There I stood. Caught like a deer in the headlights. I held my bluff. What could I say, "Oh, I'm just flexing my neck and trying to act like a Big Dog so that you'll let me tongue your ear again soon"? So, I maintained my pose. Full flex. My armpits started dripping, and I could feel my neck muscles cramping up.

"Like what?" I mumbled, bobbing my head up and down, faking a "What kind of stupid question is that?" look.

"Like that, Rick. You're standing funny. You look tense or something," she said. I tried to look unaffected, nonchalant, sort of intensely sullen, like Marlon Brando in *On the Waterfront*. I continued bobbing my head around all the while, looking from side to side, then up to the sky, then back to her. A ploy. My feeble attempt to debunk her half-baked notion that I was anything less than naturally natural. Then our eyes met. The moment of truth. She wasn't fooled.

Panicked and embarrassed, I froze. My gonads skittered upward, seeking shelter. My Big Dog act was on the line. My manhood was on the chopping block and the axe was in Sally's hand. It was fight, flight, or fess-up time. Fessing up was out of the question. I sighed, threw my head back, and sort of rolled my eyes. It worked for Brando; it could work for me. "I gotta split," I said. Then I turned and headed slowly for my car. It seemed like a very long walk.

Walking and trying to look relaxed while flexing one's neck with all one's might takes finesse. Opening a car door, getting in, and starting the car while staying flexed takes uncommon concentration.

Things were never the same with Sally and me after that. She had seen right through me, probably not for the first time, but it was the first time I had seen her see right through me. I couldn't stand it. What if she saw that I was just a clumsy, scared 16-year-old kid wrapped in a muscled-up suit of armor with big biceps and a tense neck? What if she saw that I wasn't a Big Dog at all? So from then on, I flexed harder every time I was with Sally. Not just with my neck, but with my whole psyche. Before a comment left my lips, I sanded it smooth of any sign of gentleness. I think I was even rude some of the time. And remember, I liked her. I really liked her.

Soon, it became no fun for me or for her. I flexed so hard that the love and the like in my heart got cramped. It couldn't get out. Before long, I just faded right out of Sally's life and she out of mine. It's hell on a relationship if you're flexing all the time.

I counsel a lot of people who are involved with relationships that are important to them. I've noticed that often, relationships begin with a covert agreement between two people that sounds something like this:

> **"I promise to help you convince yourself that you are the way you want to think you are, if you will promise to do the same for me."**

Actors and actresses tend to seek each other out and perform plays together. They rarely say aloud that this is what they're doing, but it is. I've seen several variations on the "knight in shining armor meets damsel in distress" theme. The first scene is often terrific, but the whole thing begins to get unpleasantly intense when one or the other gets tired of acting or sees through the other's act.

When this happens, there is often disappointment, resentment, and defensiveness about the deterioration of one's own act or the act of one's partner. As anxiety and anger emerge, there is the potential for a great deal of conflict and even for the demise of the relationship. Both parties' gremlins come charging out in full force, supporting those ugly fears of abandonment, pain, and death I spoke of earlier. The gremlin's dialogue may have a defensive flavor:

"S/he's holding you back."

"S/he is too difficult to please."

"S/he is unreasonable."

"S/he is no longer the person you married."

"S/he doesn't give you the emotional support you need."

"S/he's too dependent."

or a self-critical tone:

"S/he deserves more than you can give him/her."

"You're so dumb."

"You should be stronger."

"You should be less selfish."

"You'll never amount to anything."

The upside is that within all this sticky intensity is a wonderful opportunity for two people to see their acts as mere acts, and to begin to establish a relationship based on a mutual desire to be intimate, and consequently to let their natural selves meet, touch, and begin to dance.

Intimacy requires the ability to share the *natural you* with another and to experience his or her *natural self*. You cannot be intimate with another so long as your pure contact with him or her is interfered with by your act. Allowing the real you to emerge and be experienced by another involves allowing your body, your voice, your facial expressions, and your words to express you, rather than your act, your self-concept, or your habits. Removing these barriers leaves you exposed (which may be scary) and available for love and contentment (which is exciting). Excitement almost always underlies fear, and excitement is a prerequisite for fully enjoying yourself.

THE PLEASANT PERSON ACT

Acting can be fun so long as you clearly understand that you are not your act. A good act can get you some strokes, help you win friends, and help you make a living. Some of the most uptight people I know have good acts. So, *puleeze*, if you get into acting, enjoy it! Just don't take your act too seriously. You risk a feeling of real emptiness if you do. Acting should be thought of as practical, as experimentation, as a good time; even as a well-planned manipulation, as conscious pretentiousness, or

81

as entertainment. Some acts are, of course, better than others. You'll be best served to select an act that is consistent with the natural you.

The Pleasant Person Act is one of the most popular. I asked several of my clients, students, and colleagues about this act. All were aware of it, and some have used it as a base from which they have created their own unique performing style. I was surprised by the degree of agreement I found among those I consulted as to the essential attributes of the Pleasant Person Act. Here they are:

- Listen more than you talk.
- Speak softly, but audibly.
- Don't repeat yourself.
- Use no more words than are necessary.
- Make eye contact without staring.
- Pay attention to what you see.
- Don't chew your mustache (or anyone else's).
- Brush your teeth at least twice a day.
- Don't make noises when you breathe.
- Breathe fully but not heavily.
- Don't eat onions or garlic before social engagements.
- Dress in clothes that fit you and feel good.
- Sit straight but not rigid.
- Don't brag.
- Be friendly.
- Shake hands firmly but don't overdo it.
- Verbally acknowledge your discomfort when you notice it.
- Verbally acknowledge your lack of understanding when you are aware of it.

- Ask questions and reflect on the answers.
- Be kind to animals.
- Don't repeat yourself.
- Look for things to like and comment on them.
- Keep your body and hair clean.
- Make a daily checklist of things to do.

- Don't do two of them.
- Do the rest.
- Exercise several times a week.
- When having a conversation with a child, kneel down to his or her eye level.
- Don't expect children to act like adults.
- Don't call people names.
- Don't talk badly behind people's backs.
- To a third party, say something nice about someone else.

- Keep your body relaxed.
- Don't force a smile.
- Don't interrupt.
- Go slowly.
- Use a lot of simple sentences.

- Don't repeat yourself.
- Don't use a monotone.
- Use good grammar.
- Be respectful to your elders—no exceptions.
- When people visit you, make them comfortable.
- Do not wear too much cologne or perfume.
- Keep agreements.

- Respect other cultures' customs.
- Do more than your part to keep the planet clean.
- Keep the temperature comfortable in your dwelling.
- Wake up early.
- Don't pick your teeth in public.
- Cover your mouth when you cough.
- Leave well enough alone.
- Remember names.
- Don't tell ethnic jokes or make racial slurs.
- Ask clearly and explicitly for what you want.
- Take responsibility for being clearly understood.
- Listen carefully to what others say.
- Ask for clarification when you are uncertain.
- Write legibly.
- Don't ask rhetorical questions.
- Don't overeat.
- Be in the midst of learning something new.
- Accept what is obvious.
- Change your routine once a week.
- Change this routine once in a while.
- Limit your intake of sugar without being obsessive about it.
- Give up trying to be something special.
- Don't smoke.

- Don't get obviously drunk or slur your words.
- Don't physically hurt any living thing.
- When in a dialogue, get in touch with that part of you that is nosy but not intrusive, remembering that real life is far more interesting than television.

- Don't be anxious to verbalize a parallel from your own experience.
- Don't act out your joy to the point of being phony.
- Don't let your sadness turn you into the kind of grump that's a pain in the ass to be with.
- Do not use hair slick'um.
- Don't repeat yourself.

- _____
- _____
- _____

I've left some blanks here for you to list a few of your own notions relevant to the Pleasant Person Act. You might want to use this information as a basis for shoring up your own act, so make sure that what you write reflects your conscious choice and not your gremlin's *shoulds* and fears.

Remember, you're not your act.

CONCEPTS OF WHAT IS SO

You probably hold concepts not only of yourself but of other people, processes, and relationships. It is valuable in taming your gremlin to know the difference between these concepts and the things the concepts represent. As I mentioned in the preface of this book, "The word is not the thing, nor the description the described." Even more simply put, and you needn't applaud my originality: "There is no substitute for experience." Your own experience.

If your mouth were dry and your throat parched, I could say the word *water* to you for eons, and your mouth would stay dry and your throat parched. I could read you Webster's definition of water, and still you would be thirsty. I could even describe to you water's physical properties, and still your thirst would remain unquenched. But one small taste of the actual thing called "water" would aid in relieving your thirst even if you were unable to spell the word *water*, much less define it. This same analogy holds true for every object, process, and relationship, and it has relevance to the process of taming your gremlin.

As you improve your ability to center yourself and to *simply notice*, and as you continue to practice doing so, you will become increasingly conscious of your gremlin's use of concepts. Concepts can become hypnotic convictions that serve as a veil between your essence and the world as it actually exists. That is why your gremlin uses them. Direct contact with your own rich experience in

the current moment leads to excitement, and excitement is a prerequisite for experiencing the vibrancy of existence. Lack of contact will, over time, lead to boredom, and boredom is no more than a form of deadening yourself, something your gremlin loves for you to do.

As you begin to differentiate yourself from your gremlin, you will find it easier and easier to *simply notice* your veil of concepts. For goodness's sake, don't try to rid yourself of them or to argue over them with your gremlin. Grappling with your gremlin is a big mistake, even for a worthy cause.

6

Be Wary of Grappling with Your Gremlin

Becoming involved in intellectual discussions and arguments with your gremlin is to pay your gremlin far too much attention. This can be a dangerous mistake.

Your gremlin is to you as the Tar Baby was to Br'er Rabbit. He wants you to become involved with him, but every degree of involvement leads to more involvement. Your gremlin is a sticky sort, and the more you fight with him, the more enmeshed you will become in his depressive muck.

If you grapple with your gremlin, you will eventually become anxious, frustrated, and tired of the whole business at hand (regardless of the issue). You will want to drop the whole subject, but your gremlin won't let you.

Your gremlin will lead you to believe that if you continue to analyze the issue, you will eventually figure your way out of the whole entanglement. Your gremlin is cruel. A quick and common example of how grappling with your gremlin can get you into trouble is one having to do with jealousy.

In my experience counseling couples, I have encountered hundreds of jealous husbands and wives. Jealousy, like any human process, is neither innately good nor innately bad. If, however, the only payoff for jealousy is misery for the people involved, it really doesn't make much sense, now does it? Especially if one's goal is to feel good—to enjoy oneself. Many of the jealous people I counsel are uncomfortable with their jealousy on one hand, but stimulated by it on the other.

I saw a couple recently who loved one another very much. Let's call them John and Sarah. John was very upset, almost in anguish, because his wife told him that she found one of their mutual male friends "sexy." That is all she said. The comment seemed like an innocent one, even to John. But John's gremlin took hold. His gremlin tortured him with images of his wife being more attracted to the other man than to him, making love with the man, and his wife leaving him (John). As John began to open up to me, he shared that on occasion he fantasized catching his wife in a romantic encounter with the man. Eventually he realized and shared with me that he found the whole idea somehow stimulating. It didn't make him happy, but it stimulated him, sort of like scratching a rash. And that is how it is with gremlins.

Gremlins do their best to get us to settle for titillation rather than for full, rich fulfillment and contentment. John wondered for days about his wife and her intentions. In one of our joint sessions, he even talked with her about his feelings, and he shared his fears and fantasies. She gave him all the assurance one person could give another, and intellectually he believed her. However, in the days that followed, his gremlin persisted in reintroducing the disturbing questions and fantasies.

John tried over and over to resolve his thinking on the issue, and he discussed the matter several times with his wife. On occasion, he would convince himself of his wife's fidelity. He could see the misery that his gremlin was perpetuating within him and between him and his wife. They were both sick and tired of the whole issue, but John still felt compelled to think about it. He grew irritable with Sarah, and their discussions about the matter began to feel to her like interrogations. John knew that what he was doing was eroding their relationship, but he just couldn't leave the matter alone. In one of our sessions, he likened his experience to that of watching a sexy, slightly violent movie. He didn't have loving feelings while going over the confused morass of facts and fantasies his gremlin dangled before him, but he was irresistibly stimulated by them.

Your gremlin knows precisely how to get your attention, and he will create movies in your head perfectly suited to your vulnerabilities. They may be sexy, sad, violent, scary, or like beautiful fairy tales, but certainly they will be suited to capturing and holding your attention. You will find yourself dying to know the ending of the movie and forgetting that the only real ending is to leave the theater or to not take the movie so seriously. After all, it's just a movie.

The problem in this whole scenario was not Sarah's relationship with a sexy man or even John's relationship with Sarah. The toxic relationship here was the one between John and his gremlin. John was giving his gremlin far too much attention. Instead of simply noticing and hearing his gremlin's chatter, he was seriously considering what the gremlin had to say and hoping to disprove it. He was grappling with his gremlin.

John continually went over and over the facts, fantasies, and questions raised by his gremlin, hoping to think through the whole matter and arrive at a peaceful, all-conclusive, lasting resolution. A far better idea would have been to use the first step of our Gremlin-Taming Method: breathe, relax, and simply notice his gremlin's chatter without becoming involved with it. He might even have chosen to grapple with his gremlin for a while. The key word here is *chosen*.

Choosing to grapple with your gremlin is far different from being unconsciously sucked into participating in a misery-making wrestling match with him. When you grapple by choice, you retain some control over the grappling. Even by choice, to grapple with your gremlin is always a bit risky. Gremlins are tenacious, and once they have you involved with them it is difficult to escape. For this reason, I recommend that when you choose to grapple with your gremlin you do so only for a few seconds or minutes at a time, and only after setting a very precise time limit on your grappling. Make certain to stop at the end of the time period. One to five minutes is usually more than enough grappling time. Once you set the time limit ahead of time, get in there and grapple to your heart's content. Have a ball. Fantasize, analyze, ruminate, obsess, get turned on, wound up, let down, bummed out, happy, excited, scared, whatever—for a few minutes. Then stop, center yourself, and use your "I'm taming my gremlin" mantra. Remember that special place behind your heart and consider your breath passing over it and brushing gently against it.

Your gremlin is proficient at creating a cerebral house of mirrors. Even if on some rare occasion you manage to arrange the concepts in your head in such a way that you feel like you are the intellectual victor over your gremlin, be assured it will not last. Within a few minutes or, at best, a few days, he will raise the whole issue again and you will find yourself struggling desperately to resolve the whole matter all over again. Taming your gremlin has absolutely nothing to do with arguing with him. Remember also, that taming your gremlin has nothing to do with *trying* and *straining*. It is a precise method relying on:

Simply Noticing

Choosing and Playing with Options

Being in Process

As you begin to directly experience *how* you are and *who* you are, your gremlin's myths, the habits he has talked you into accepting, and the concepts he perpetuates on which these habits are based, there will occur an automatic adjustment upward in your level of contentment. Why this is so, I don't know, but it is so and it has been so forever. As I mentioned earlier, some call this phenomenon the "Zen Theory of Change." Here it is again:

I free myself not by trying to be free but by *simply noticing* how I am imprisoning myself in the very moment I am imprisoning myself.

7

Ushering Your
Habits and Concepts
into the Light

Completing the exercise that follows will be helpful in clueing you in to some of the habits and concepts your gremlin may be using to confine you. Simply relax, breathe, and enjoy yourself while you play within the context of the following experiment. It is unnecessary to work at it or to strain.

YOUR EARLY DAZE

Allow yourself to remember for a moment a house in which you lived between the ages 3 and 7. If you lived in more than one house during that time, choose the one about which you have the warmest feeling. Create a "houseplan"-style drawing of the dwelling (as if you were above it, looking down). If phrases such as "I'm a terrible artist" or "I hate to draw" fly through your head, notice them and then let them go. These are concepts your gremlin is feeding you. He's tricky. Simply relax and sketch your house as you remember it. For goodness' sake, don't worry about precise proportions or layout. Here as an example is a drawing of the house I grew up in:

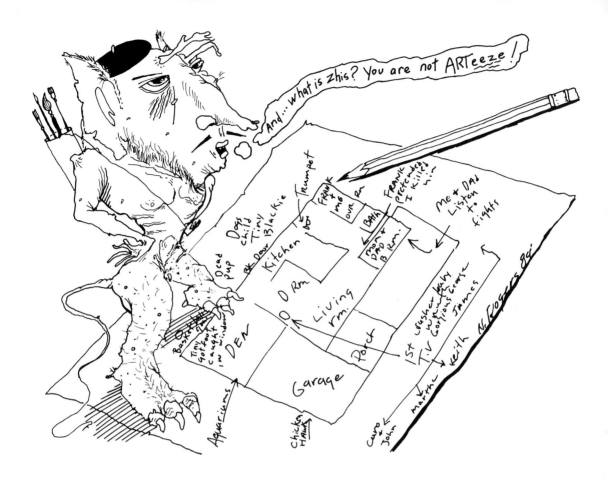

Now, just for a moment, allow yourself to reflect on each room in the house. Jot down key words and/or draw symbols in each room relevant to your memories of being in that room.

Remember that these need make sense to no one but you, and remember also that there is absolutely no way to do this wrong. Enjoy the process. You may be surprised at how much or how little you remember. You may recall pictures that hung on the wall, a design on the floor tile or carpeting, furniture, or even molding around doors. How much or how little you remember is of no real importance. It is no better to recall lots of details than to recall only a few. This is not a test. It is an exercise, and it is being offered to you in the interest of self-exploration and enjoyment. Relax. Go slowly.

Allow yourself to remember each room. You may recall aromas, a general feeling, or even a color associated with a given room. You probably will become aware of variations in your physical experience as you let your awareness move from room to room. Simply notice your emotions and thoughts as you do this, jotting down a few words or symbols as reminders of your memories.

As for me, at this moment I am remembering the feeling of lying next to my father in my parents' bedroom. We were listening to a boxing match on the radio. I remember how good my dad smelled and how warm his flannel pajamas were as I lay next to him. I think that Ezzard Charles was boxing. I don't know that I ever thought about this experience before, but at this moment it seems it was extremely pleasurable. I was very happy there next to him.

While living in the house you've drawn, you had a vast number of experiences, and from these experiences you formed many ideas about who you are, about relationships, and about the nature of existence. Learning that occurs experientially is very deep-seated. It is as if the learning is in our bones rather than simply in our intellect. Often our experiential learnings and the beliefs we form as a result of them are outside of our awareness. They are so much a part of us that to step back and objectively view them is difficult, yet they affect us day in and day out in every conceivable situation.

In order for you to become a bit more aware of beliefs and habits you formed while living in this house, I have included below some items to which you can respond. Relax as you read each item and be honest with yourself. Respond to these items based on what you saw and heard, not on what you were told.

From what you experienced in this house, what did you learn about:

The expression of love _____

_____

Physical stroking such as hugging and kissing _____

_____

How anger is handled _____

_____

How decisions are made _____

_____

The expression of sadness _____

_____

The expression of joy _____

_____

Trust _____

_____

Honesty _____

_____

How men are _____

_____

How women are _____

_____

How smart you are _____

_____

How capable a leader you are _____

_____

About your athletic abilities _____

_____

About your creative abilities _____

_____

How lovable you are _____

_____

How likeable you are _____

_____

How attractive you are _____

_____

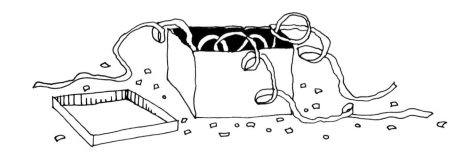

Look back over your responses to all of the above items and consider them as representative of a few of the concepts according to which you have tended to lead your life. As you look at each of these learnings, you might ask yourself, "Do I still lead my life in accordance with these ideas?" If so, you might ask, "Does this learning have value in my life today? Does it take into account who I am today? Is this learning one I have altered over time? Is this learning one I wish to reconsider from this point forward?"

In order to answer these questions, let's carry our experiment a little further. The following fill-in-the-blank items will help you become aware of some of the concepts of yourself you may still be living *within*.

Use first-level thought in responding to them. First-level thought is the simple process of gently reflecting on any given topic during a couple of easy, complete breaths. It's a superior alternative to fretting and worry and at times is more efficient than in-depth analytical thinking. First-level thought involves your innate ability to come forth with useful information quickly and effortlessly, and is especially valuable in learning about yourself and getting in touch with your most fundamental emotions, concepts, and preferences.

WHAT YOU THINK OF YOU

Simply take a couple of full clear breaths while allowing your mind to focus on each item below. Trust your first-level thought. Your answers are between you and you, and need only be true for you *here* and *now*. Be honest. It's important to be settled down and relaxed to give this activity your best shot. Remember what you've learned about choice, and if you're not enthusiastic about responding to these items now, don't. When you're ready, get some paper and something to write with and dive into the experience.

I am incredibly _____.

I am a lousy _____.

I am _____ intelligent.

I have a knack for _____.

I am extremely good at _____.

I am a(n) _____ athlete.

Most folks who really know me think that I am

_____.

I will never learn to _____.

I am a run-of-the-mill _____.

Stick with what comes up first. Don't argue with it, just note it and jot it down. Every answer you are jotting down is an idea. That is all—an idea, a concept, a belief, an image, an intangible bit of hullabaloo. *But* it's an intangible bit of hullabaloo that is powerfully hypnotic, and if it's left to lie unnoticed in your unconscious, it will permeate your experience and dictate your future. The hypnotic images in your mind predispose your reactions to your experiences in life. Self-hypnosis is as constant and perpetual a process for human beings as is breathing. So if your desire is to become an exemplary player at the game of life, it's time to straighten up, fly right, and give yourself a fair and square shot at being the best you can be and at having the best time you can have. A shot based on who you are now—not on who you decided to be in the old days. It's time to become aware of your concepts. It's time to become aware of your hypnotic convictions.

Your responses on the items above and those that follow will give you some important clues as to how you may be limiting or aiding your pleasure and productivity. Let's continue now.

My life is _____.

My future is going to be _____.

I would rather be _____.

I am far too _____.

Come on. Be honest. It's more important to trust your first-level thought than to paint a nice picture.

As a lover, I am _____.

My body is _____.

My health is _____.

I am _____ to look at.

I am _____ prosperous.

By bringing prevalent beliefs about yourself into the foreground of your conscious mind as you've just done, you've already begun to lessen their hypnotic control over you. Remember the Zen Theory of Change we discussed earlier:

I free myself not by trying to be free, but by *simply noticing* how I am imprisoning myself in the very moment I am imprisoning myself.

Every time you *simply notice* one of your gremlin's less-than-positive tapes, especially if you do so *as the tape is playing*, you can attend to it with a sense of relaxed detachment, even with humor, and you can choose your response. This gives the *natural you* a chance to evaluate the tape's value in the context of the present situation. You needn't strain to change or waste time delving into your past to ferret out the tape's origin. Just relax and place your awareness on the message. Really attend to it. Turn up the volume on it for a few moments. Hear it but don't take it too seriously. Do this on a few occasions. Before long the message on the tape, if it is untrue, outdated, or simply no longer beneficial to you, will begin to fade in intensity.

Your gremlin will attack you with fear tactics in the form of catastrophic predictions and painful memories in an effort to keep self-limiting concepts and habits in place. Follow his lead and you'll feel blah from repeating the same behaviors over and over again, blue from feeling that no one knows the real you, or bottled up from over-censoring true expressions of yourself.

The *natural you*, on the other hand, is masterful at modifying self-limiting and counterproductive thoughts and traits once you bring them and your gremlin's wailing out of the shadows. The brighter the light you shine on old fears, outdated beliefs, and cumbersome habitual behaviors, the better the *natural you,* the *observer,* can see the absurdity in them.

Later, when we discuss playing with options, we will explore other strategies for foiling your gremlin. For now, know that:

Simply noticing is a powerful tool.

REALITY AND DUALITY

As you begin to notice your habits and the concepts on which your habits are based, your gremlin will insist that they are necessary to your well-being. He may do this by raising an all-out ruckus and by making demands, by frightening you with catastrophic expectations of the future, by reminding you of the nasty consequences of your actions in past situations when you did not listen to him, and even by gently putting his arm around you and convincing you that he has your best interest at heart. Regardless of how he presents himself, he is your gremlin and his view of "what is so" is grounded in make-believe. Be aware of him. It is unnecessary to *try* to ignore him or to fight him. Simply notice him. From your vantage point of being centered, you will be able to hear his chatter. Listen to it, and think of it as just chatter. Remember—to grapple with your gremlin is to lose to your gremlin. At the point you begin fighting with your gremlin, you are in what I call a state of duality.

Taming your gremlin requires that you be in reality, not in duality. When you are in reality, your energy flows freely within you and is available to you for your use in relating to the world. Here is a simple conceptualization of a person feeling whole and in reality rather than in duality:

102

When you feel this sort of wholeness, you are more sensitive to your environment, including the people in it, and to your physical body. You can perceive, love, problem-solve, create, and even fight close to your full potential. You have your full energy available to you in this state, and consequently you can more fully enjoy this life. When, on the other hand, your energy is tied up in an internal conflict, i.e., a duality, you don't have much energy left over to experience and enjoy your body, your life, or the world around you.

In this state of being, you will feel anxious and/or disgruntled and/or bottled-up and/or empty. In short—you will not enjoy yourself. Your gremlin prefers you to stay in a state of duality. Here is a conceptualization of a person in duality:

Let me remind you to do yourself a favor and simply read and enjoy this book. Do not, I repeat, do not try to figure out anything. The real you understands what you have read. No analysis is necessary. Relax and breathe. If you get confused and/or distracted, simply stop for a while.

TIPS FOR SIMPLY NOTICING YOUR GREMLIN

An undetected gremlin can create asthma, heart attacks, ulcers, colitis, headaches, backaches, neuroses, psychoses, and just about any other malady you can imagine. You, however, have nothing to worry about so long as you are able to *simply notice* him. Be very specific about noticing any tension in your body, for this will clue you to your gremlin's presence.

If, for example, you notice that your breathing is shallow, pay attention to exactly how shallow it is. If your neck is tight, what muscles does the tightness cover? How tight is your neck? If you have a headache, how deep into your skull does the pain go? What are the parameters of the pain? Can you imagine a color that describes the pain? What might the color be? *Simply notice* your body and the effect of your gremlin on it. As you *simply notice*, these effects will become more and more evident, as will your gremlin himself. Analysis, judgment, and attempts to change are unnecessary.

For the next few days, key in on where tension makes itself known in your body. Notice your jaws, shoulders, neck, head, back, genitals, and stomach. Notice the effect of tension on your breathing. Listen for your gremlin's chatter when you detect these symptoms. Notice how your gremlin is scaring you and/or what he is saying to you about you. Shine a bright light on his musings and/or his all-out verbal abuse, and make a choice to attend to it for a limited period or to direct your awareness elsewhere.

When your gremlin is really working on you, he will shadow you to such an extent that it will feel as though you are absorbed by him. During these times it will seem as if you become him. As your gremlin, you will feel self-righteous, defensive, greedy, and even downright mean. Your attitude toward others will be defensive and manipulative. You will have an inordinate investment in making certain you are not taken advantage of. Your body may feel tight, and this tension may manifest itself in a furrowed brow, a headache, an upset stomach, or simply a mild tension. Your thoughts may become extremely rapid. The power with which your gremlin will be attempting to squelch your essence and the natural you may be so intense that you may not even notice him unless you allow yourself the sort of self-awareness we practiced earlier. Use what you have learned about centering yourself.

Reflect on and practice what you are learning. Remember to:

Breathe.

Center yourself.

Use your "I'm taming my gremlin" mantra.

Notice where you end and all else begins—your skin.

Establish the *here* and *now* as a home base from which you shine your spotlight of awareness.

Use your spotlight of awareness to *simply notice*:
- Your body
- The world that surrounds you
- Your habits
- Your concepts
- Your gremlin's chatter

While it is counterproductive to force yourself to change a habitual behavior pattern or a concept, it can be very productive to experiment with change once in a while. In the Gremlin-Taming Method, this step is called *playing with options*.

8

Choosing and Playing with Options

I want to emphasize the word *playing* in *playing with options*. Playing implies enjoying yourself, and that is precisely what I mean here. Experimenting with change can be scary. When you change a habitual way of responding to emotions and to life circumstances, you really won't know if you're going to get roses or rotten tomatoes. As I've mentioned, however, underneath your fear is probably excitement. If you can enjoy the excitement and unpredictability inherent in letting go of those habitual responses and the concepts on which they are based, your Gremlin-Taming Method will be a smooth one.

Enjoying the process is an integral part of taming your gremlin. Your gremlin would have you believe that feeling good requires working hard, straining, gutting up, trying, analyzing, grunting, groaning, working things out, and most of all worrying. The truth is, there is no positive cause-effect correlation between the action implied by any of these terms and gaining a genuine sense of simple peace and contentment.

Your sense of inner contentment and satisfaction will increase as you enhance your gremlin-taming abilities; that is, as you become more adept at *simply noticing* your body, the world around you, your habits for responding to your emotions and to life circumstances, and your concepts; *choosing and playing with options*; and being *in process*.

If you are aware of telling yourself you *should* change, your gremlin has got you buffaloed. *Should, ought,* and *must* are gremlin terms that dampen the spirit of experimentation. Instead, simply change for a change. Play around. As you become aware of an outdated concept or an old habitual behavior, consider playing with changing the behavior. Change for the moment. To vow to change forever sets you up for a gremlin attack, since that wily master of misery will turn your vow into a *should* with which to beat you over the head. To vow to change forever would be no more than to develop a new habit or a new act. Granted, it may be a more constructive habit or act than the one you were using, but any habit or act can limit your potential for leading a creative, enjoyable life. Again, the key word is *choice.*

BEING AT CHOICE

To be at choice from situation to situation and from moment to moment is vitally important in taming your gremlin.

On occasion I've met people who've had a little counseling. A little counseling is like a little knowledge of karate. It can get you into bad trouble. Here is a common scenario:

A woman goes into counseling and becomes aware of her lifelong tendency to repress her anger. Her newfound awareness is so exciting that she develops a new rule.

Instead of thinking that she should not express anger, she now fervently believes that she should always show her anger. She has developed what I call an "inverted" neurosis and is no better off than before. Her gremlin, waiting in the wings, will either continue to badger her about how awful her anger is or, with a sudden shift in tactics, he will begin to berate her each time she is not totally honest about her feelings of anger, telling her that she *should* be. Remember:

Taming your gremlin does not require developing new *shoulds*. Instead,

Simply Notice

Choose and Play with Options

Be in Process

For example, if your gremlin has convinced you that certain of your emotions are dangerous or wrong or that you're not entitled to them, you may feel panicky when you feel these emotions. If, on the other hand, your gremlin has convinced you that some powerful emotions are physically intolerable and will hurt you when you hold them in, he may encourage you to express them immediately and without respect for others. You may feel better for the moment, but in the long run your gremlin will win by setting you up to feel anxious, guilty, isolated, or empty. Respect your gremlin's trickiness.

BREATHE AND FULLY EXPERIENCE

If, instead of listening to your gremlin, you will simply breathe, feel your emotions, and give them lots of space in your body, you will notice that these emotions are no more than simple energy, and to experience energy is to feel vibrant and alive. After all, emotions are intended to be felt and fully experienced and used to benefit your existence. Anger is not inherently evil, sadness does not automatically imply depression, sexual feelings don't automatically engender promiscuity, joy is not the same as irresponsibility and foolishness, and fear does not equal cowardice. The only time that emotions become dangerous is when we habitually bottle them up or discharge them impulsively without respect for other living things.

Emotions will not disappear simply because you don't acknowledge or express them. By the same token, it is unnecessary to express every emotion outwardly. As you begin to pay closer and closer attention to your emotions and to their effects on your body, you will notice that there is nothing in an emotion to be afraid of. It is only your gremlin who is afraid of your emotions, because he knows that when you are experiencing them fully, without judgment, you feel a simple sense of vibrancy, and that feeling of vibrancy is the key to fully enjoying your gift of life.

Your gremlin would prefer that you focus your attention on him instead of simply experiencing your emotions. Often, in what appears to be an intense situation, if you take the time to relax and *simply notice* what you are feeling, reminding yourself that you do not have to do anything with your emotions and that emotions are not dangerous, you will experience a sense of *relaxed power*. This sense has been described many ways, including feeling self-actualized, integrated, whole, happy, loving, centered, in the zone, high, good, and hunky-dory. As you take the time to simply experience the physical sensations known as emotions, you will begin to enjoy them more and more. Choosing options for what to do with them will become easier and more enjoyable. It may even feel like an adventure.

Again, one of the most commonly overlooked options is to give your emotion of the moment lots of space within you. That is, to

breathe and fully experience.

Another option is to

change for a change.

CHANGE FOR A CHANGE

When you decide to express outwardly a particular emotion, it makes sense for you to select an option for doing so that leaves you feeling good on the inside and at the same time gets you what you want from your environment. The process for selecting these kinds of options is what makes taming your gremlin an enjoyable adventure, for here is where you can be creative. You will be surprised at the options you can think of for expressing yourself once you get into *choosing and playing with options*.

On occasion, you might select options that you consider to be consistent with your personality (or your act of the moment). At other times, you might select options that are totally out of character for you. So what? Be out of character. Being out of character might help you blow your act, and by now you recognize the minimal value of your act anyway. Play.

If your tendency has been to behave timidly when given a compliment, consider playing with another option. The next time someone so much as implies it's good to know you, take a deep breath and enjoy the moment. You might even announce, "That feels good! Tell me more." Change for a change. Fool around.

If, when in conflict with others, your habit has been to scare yourself into stifling your anger, look your fear squarely in the eye and ask yourself what's the worst that can happen if you express yourself. Consider honestly describing your current experience. You might, for example, try out your version of one or any combination of these statements:

"There is something that I want to say to you, but I'm afraid that you will throw a fit. Are you willing to hear me out?"

"I'm angry with you. What is also true is that I respect you and value our relationship."

"You're important to me and I want us to remain friends, *and* there are some things you're doing that are driving me nuts."

"I'm hesitant to talk with you about a certain sensitive issue, but I don't like feeling what I'm feeling and would like to clear the air. Are you open to a frank discussion?"

"I'd like you to hear all of what I am about to say to you and really consider it before you respond."

"I want to really listen to you and I want you to listen to me."

"This may be a tough conversation for us because my tendency may be to talk ugly and yours may be to give me that sneer of yours. As we have this conversation, let's make an effort to treat each other with love and respect."

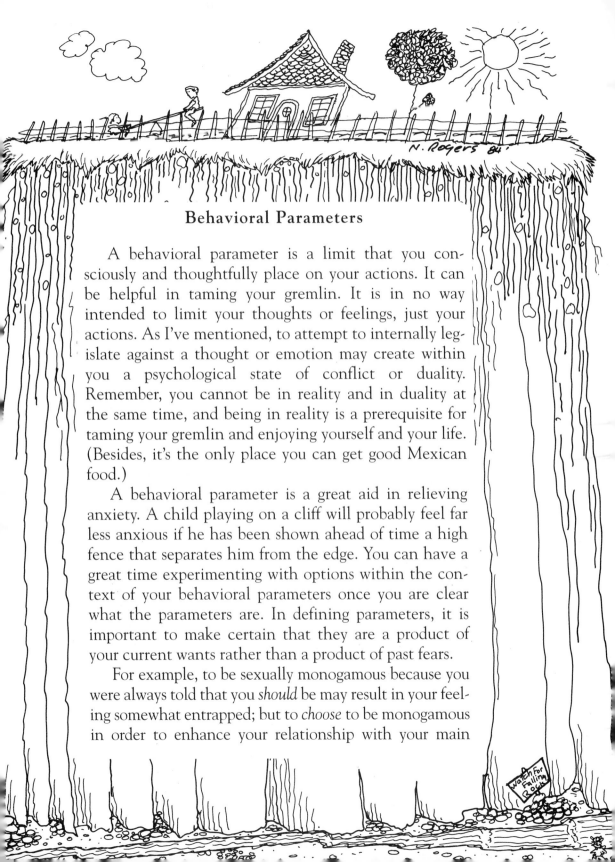

Behavioral Parameters

A behavioral parameter is a limit that you consciously and thoughtfully place on your actions. It can be helpful in taming your gremlin. It is in no way intended to limit your thoughts or feelings, just your actions. As I've mentioned, to attempt to internally legislate against a thought or emotion may create within you a psychological state of conflict or duality. Remember, you cannot be in reality and in duality at the same time, and being in reality is a prerequisite for taming your gremlin and enjoying yourself and your life. (Besides, it's the only place you can get good Mexican food.)

A behavioral parameter is a great aid in relieving anxiety. A child playing on a cliff will probably feel far less anxious if he has been shown ahead of time a high fence that separates him from the edge. You can have a great time experimenting with options within the context of your behavioral parameters once you are clear what the parameters are. In defining parameters, it is important to make certain that they are a product of your current wants rather than a product of past fears.

For example, to be sexually monogamous because you were always told that you *should* be may result in your feeling somewhat entrapped; but to *choose* to be monogamous in order to enhance your relationship with your main squeeze may be invigorating. Recall that the overall process for taming your gremlin is to *simply notice; be at choice and play with options;* and *be in process.* As for *playing with options,* thus far we've discussed two:

Breathe and fully experience

Change for a change

ACCENTING THE OBVIOUS

Let's explore yet another option for you to play with. Let's call this option *accenting the obvious.* Remember, the brighter the light you shine on old fears, outdated ideas, and cumbersome habits, the better you can detect the absurdity in them. To have some fun exposing antiquated notions and beliefs, think of ways to accentuate them. Fritz Perls, a truly brilliant psychiatrist and teacher, was a whiz when it came to accenting the obvious. He was one of several pioneers who developed a potent psychotherapeutic approach known today as gestalt therapy.

Fritz Perls's approach was efficient and effective primarily because it was existential—dealing with the client's experience in the here and now; phenomenological—leading people to observe and experience how they tended to feel, think, and behave, rather than why; and experiential—vividly accenting the client's habitual behaviors and the concepts on which they were based so that they could be felt and observed with an attitude of "creative indifference."

You can use this same sort of existential, experiential, phenomenological approach to enhance your own life. To do so, simply notice and accent the obvious—to the point of absurdity, if you wish. Experiment with forming a mental picture of yourself acting out your feelings. If, for example, you observe yourself shrinking from a conflict or hiding from a challenge, try forming a mental picture of yourself acting out your feelings. Imagine yourself growing smaller and smaller, or trembling with fear, or hiding or cowering in a dark closet, or better yet—if the situation affords you the opportunity—actually scrunch up your posture, or put your head down or go hide in a closet or walk like you have your tail between your legs. Give the natural you the chance to observe the strange behavior and the belief on which it is based.

Be creative and playful with the process of accenting the obvious. If, for example, you notice yourself holding your anger in to the point that you feel like a thundercloud, accent the feeling. Hold your breath, puff up real big, then go look at yourself in a mirror. And don't overlook one of the simplest ways to accent the obvious— that is, to describe verbally to someone else what you are noticing about yourself (in the very moment you're noticing it.) Say, for example,

"I'm really filled with fury right now and I feel myself holding it all inside and puffing up like a thundercloud."

Or, let's say your gremlin is putting you down— implying you are incapable or unworthy, for example. Accent his chatter by speaking it aloud or turning up the volume on it. Make up a gremlin voice if you want. Often you will see the absurdity in your gremlin's diatribe. Go all out as you give play to his monologue. It might be something like this: "You miserable lowlife. You'll never amount to anything. Your commitment to mediocrity is staggering. I'm not sure you could even work your way up to 'so-so.' Give it up. Even those close to you are getting fed up. You're gonna end up old and alone and living in an alley getting gnawed on by rats."

Even if your gremlin's put-downs and scary taunts have an element of truth in them, as you accentuate your gremlin's chatter you will become quite aware of the absurdity inherent in choosing to spend precious moments of your limited life listening to him.

Simply noticing the message your gremlin is sending your way *in the moment that the message is playing* gives you some distance, not just from the message but from that monster of the mind—your very own personal gremlin.

Your gremlin is not just the self-limiting messages in your head. He's the force that brings them forth.

Your gremlin has a purpose—your demise—and he moves with forthright intention. Your gremlin is the macabre master of misery, the demon of distress. He will use the data in your mental storehouse to squelch your potential for pleasure and productivity, dampen your creativity, weaken your body, and poison your relationships. But you've got him whipped. Completely whipped. Not once and for all, but in each unique situation in which he flares up and snarls at you. All you have to do is to *simply notice* him with a sense of detachment and *choose and play with options*. So now we have three options to play with:

Breathe and fully experience

Change for a change

Accent the obvious

The following is another option:

JUST IMAGINE IT

There is a great deal of emphasis nowadays on the belief or at least the possibility that if you can imagine something, you can have it.

It's a lie. At least it's not true in my experience, and I've given the theory a first-class run for its money. That's not to say that positive visualization and positive self-talk cannot do wonders in your life. They can. I, for one, have benefited from and appreciate the work and wisdom of Bernie Siegel, as reported in his book *Love, Medicine, and Miracles,* and the work of other pioneers in the field of creative visualization, such as Carl and Stephanie Simonton. But as for me, I tend to run headlong into limits—maybe because I believe there are limits. I'm not sure. A former client of mine named Joanne described the dilemma aptly.

Joanne and her husband Glenn were deeply involved, not just with one another, but with an organization to which they belonged. The organization sponsored an ongoing series of personal growth seminars that Joanne and Glenn attended weekly. Some of these were evening events, and others were workshops that lasted for several days. Throughout the time I counseled Joanne and Glenn, they continued to participate in these events and made some very positive changes. As individuals, they were expanding their boundaries (and their jargon), but circumstances in their marriage were still far less than rosy. In one of our sessions, Joanne expressed her fear that their marriage would fall apart, to which Glenn replied, "Joanne, if you hold in your mind that our marriage will fall apart, our marriage *will* fall apart." Joanne looked at Glenn calmly and then asked, simply, "Well, Glenn, if I hold in my mind that our dog, Rags, will crap gold nuggets, will he?"

Joanne has a way with words, and I offer these particular ones to you simply as a way of saying that while, in my opinion, creative visualization is among the most exciting options you and I have for promoting positive change in our lives, it's a good idea to balance it with some constructive thought, some hard work, and some good choices.

In my experience, it is absolutely true that people whose lives are filled with love, prosperity, and contentment are people who like themselves, believe in their hearts that they deserve the best, and who see in their mind's eye their lives evolving positively. These folks, however, also tend to be people who are willing to take the time and make the effort to plan constructively and to do the work necessary to get them where they want to be.

If you carefully plan your steps to get from point A to point B, and if your steps are realistic, and if you put one foot in front of the other to take the steps, you will in all likelihood get where you want to go. When I help my clients with the process of bringing about the circumstances they wish to create in their lives, I focus with them on breaking antiquated, self-limiting concepts of who they are and what they can accomplish, on creating an image of where they want to be and on *planning and doing*.

Modifying, and in some cases throwing away, deep-rooted but outdated pre-convictions is a challenging undertaking because it is so personal a process, and because it has to go on right inside your very own cranium. Let's play with this option of *just imagining* it for a moment.

Writing Your Own Script

Review your responses to the fill-in-the-blank items on page 99. Take note of those items you see as having a less than positive influence on you. Play with rewriting one or more of them in the form of an ultra-positive, affirmative monologue. Imagine that you are creating for yourself a script for a subliminal program that is going to be used in your own self-hypnosis. Don't be shy about plugging in responses that make your life seem finer than you've ever dreamed possible. Do so even if it feels as if you're telling yourself a bundle of outrageous, self-glorifying lies. Elaborate and do so in your own words.

In your rewriting, use words that fit for you rather than rote declarations. It's been my experience—and my clients and students have supported this notion—that going on a positive tirade in your head is more fun and produces more rapid qualitative results than one-sentence affirmations such as "I am very intelligent" or "I am loving and wise." Get into the process. Be indulgent. Where positive self-talk is concerned, restraint is a bad idea. Go on for moments on end if you choose.

For example, on the third item if you originally wrote "I am *fairly* intelligent," you might now write, "I am smart as a whip and quick-witted to boot. I get a real kick out of how quickly I learn. I'm getting sharper with every breath. It's a blast to be fast."

Don't merely tell yourself that you will become more intelligent, but rather that you are already brilliant, that at this moment you are becoming more so, that the process will continue, that you deserve to grow wiser, and that it is a done deal that is right now manifesting and pervading every aspect of your life. You can do the same with remarkable results regarding your sex appeal, your lovability, your likeability, your relationships, your health, and even your income.

Do this sort of reworking with all of the items to which your responses were obviously self-limiting, and use the information you draft as a basis for a conversation with yourself. Trot it out and play it loud and proud every chance you get. You might even want to create an actual recording to play from time to time.

Once you've created your script, embellish the process by creating images of yourself feeling and doing exactly as you would like, and of your life working just the way you want it to. Be unrelenting. Create positive images, then conjure them up and give them a concentrated look-see every chance you get.

This is a very personal and private process, so milk it for all it's worth. You can use what you write as the basis for an internal program designed to fill your life with more pleasure and less pain than you thought likely. You can do it. And it's well worth the effort.

Now I know that stick-in-the-mud gremlin of yours thinks this power of positive thinking stuff is all a bunch of frothy guff. But if your self-awareness is up to snuff, you'll notice that listening to your gremlin feels a helluva lot worse than affirmative self-talk. And it's a damn sight worse for you. Shattering old concepts and replacing them with affirmative inner talk and images toward the goal of sweetening your very own life not only feels good, but is good for you. *Used in conjunction with common sense and planning and doing, it can make for a noble transformation.*

Settle into some affirmative heart-to-hearts with yourself, if only briefly, every day for ten days. Center yourself and then give the process a wholehearted go. Even if you feel phony for a few seconds at the beginning of each stint, just stick with it. Soon you will feel yourself settle into the experience. Consider the ten-day period a test run, and evaluate the results. If the process starts feeling like homework, drop it for a while. When you're ready, pick up the challenge and get into it. Notice not just the long-term effects but the pleasure that emerges as you dabble within the process.

So let's review some of the options you have to play with either by themselves or in various combinations:

Breathe and fully experience

Change for a change

Accent the obvious

Just imagine it

And here's another:

REVISIT AND RE-DECIDE

If you take a good look at your outdated concepts and self-limiting habits and reflect on their origins, you will probably notice that you have formed beliefs and behaviors from your trials and errors as you've boogied and bungled through life, from what you were told as a child by those you thought knew more than you, and from what you witnessed in the attitudes and actions of prominent players in your world.

Way back when you were an innocent, eager slip of a pup, your mind thirstily lapped up experiences. You slurped down beliefs and behaviors from the folks you spent the most time observing—your mom and dad among them. I hope you had the gift of parents with a wealth of honorable intentions and common sense, but even if they were top of the line, they were human and therefore probably periodically trotted out some of their more unflattering traits right before your little peepers. You drank in the less than admirable along with the terrific, day after day. Here's a simple experiment to help you gain some insight into some of the impressions you may have unthinkingly gulped down.

Unveiling Your Veil of Concepts

Based on your past experiences, your gremlin has mesmerized you into forming concepts about self and the world. He then wove these concepts into a veil of *hypnotic convictions* through which you view everything, including yourself. He did so and does so to limit the vibrancy inherent in your having your own fresh experience of your natural self.

Make a list of ten words and short phrases that describe your parent of the same gender as you experienced him/her when you were a child. (You can learn a great deal from doing this with either parent.)

Imagine, as you create your list of adjectives and descriptive phrases, that your goal is to give me a feeling for the kind of person that parent was when you were a child. You might, for example, reflect on how your father presented himself to the world; what was important to him; how he managed his emotions of anger, joy, and sadness; how he expressed or withheld affection; how physically affectionate he was; how he handled difficult situations in his life; any prominent personality characteristics or physical traits he had; something about his value system; and anything else that you imagine would give me a feeling for how you experienced him when you were a child.

While the reckless and featherbrained may be tempted to read further now, the wise and pure-hearted will read no further before having written his or her list.

Parent of Same Gender's Characteristics	✓	−	+	M
1. _____				
2. _____				
3. _____				
4. _____				
5. _____				
6. _____				
7. _____				
8. _____				
9. _____				
10. _____				

Having now done so, look over your list of your parent's characteristics and ask yourself which of these qualities you have taken on as your own. Be honest with yourself. It doesn't matter if you like the qualities, loathe them, or are indifferent to them. If they fit you, even a little, place a check mark in the column labeled "✓."

Now look at those qualities you've checked, and ask yourself which ones you'd like to do away with. For those, put a check in the minus (−) sign column. For those qualities you'd like to keep, enjoy, and perhaps embellish, put a check in the plus (+) column. For each

one you'd like to make more useful to you by modifying or reworking, put a check in the **M** column.

The last category (the **M** column) may need some clarification. Here's an example: A client of mine, Russell, recently discovered he has inherited what he calls his dad's "pushiness." He says he wants to modify this quality by keeping his father's assertiveness and his forthrightness when it comes to standing up for himself, but he wants to eliminate the brash insensitivity to others he saw in his dad and sometimes witnesses in himself. By bringing this quality into his awareness and noting it as one he wishes to modify, Russell has already begun to lessen its hypnotic hold on him.

To enhance his process of personal growth, Russell can *simply notice* his tendency toward *pushiness* as it is occurring, and he can *simply notice* the concepts playing through his mind at those moments. He may, for example, note that he tends to be *pushy* when he feels vulnerable, when his *in charge* act is on the line, or when his gremlin has him frightened of being rejected or abandoned. Having noticed this, he can play with options. He might, for example, relax, breathe, and feel his pushiness (his belief that he needs to have his way and the bodily experience that accompanies it). Or he might accent his gremlin chatter (probably something about the necessity to control others or else get hurt), or even his own pushiness. He can change for a change if he chooses, and experiment with modifying the behavior, going overboard perhaps, by being placating or even self-effacing. The main thing is that he *simply notice, be at choice*, and *play with options*.

Via an intense experiential version of the exercise you've just completed, Sharon, a participant in one of my recent seminars, became quite certain that while she deeply loved, truly liked, and much admired her mother, she had assimilated from her one particularly disturbing tendency. Sharon became aware that, like her mother, she was often *harried*. She tended to overwhelm herself with things to do and to scurry about feeling anxious, certain she would never complete all that she had to do. Sharon noticed that this was most true for her when she was at her office and her workday was drawing to a close. At these times, Sharon's thoughts usually became scattered and rapid, her breathing shallow and fast, and, like her mother, she moved in a fashion she termed as "jerky and frenetic."

Consumed with worry during these times, Sharon became insensitive to what was going on around her and often misplaced things. She was unintentionally curt and sometimes downright rude to her coworkers. Sharon quickly discovered that she had incorporated this behavior by observing her mom, who believed that a woman's value was tied solely to the degree of activity she was engaged in, and that having too much to do and suffering about it was somehow noble. Sounds like our old friend the Grim Reaper, profiled in chapter 2, was on the scene. Sharon told me she wanted to make an effort to give up this behavior and the concept on which it was based.

I suspect that Sharon will be quite successful at modifying her tendency toward a helter-skelter mindset. After all, she's already brought it into her awareness, activating the Zen Theory of Change you and I discussed earlier, and she can expedite the change she desires by simply noticing her tendency to scurry about as the tendency manifests in her actual workday. She can *simply notice* the "I have to produce to be worthwhile" concept playing in her head and give it whatever power she chooses. She can even accentuate this notion or her harried state to the point of absurdity. And she can change for a change, exploring such options as modifying her breathing, slowing down and smoothing out her movements, focusing on one issue at a time, and taking the time to come out of the world of mind long enough to notice the sensations within her body and to notice the world around her.

You can use the information you have gathered from reflecting on your parent to enrich your life and fashion your style of being. Focus on one characteristic for two or three days. Clearly decide what part you want the characteristic to play in your life. You might decide to embellish it, lessen it, or eliminate it entirely. The keys to effective change using this method are to:

- **Stay conscious of what part you want the characteristic to play in your life.**
- *Simply notice* **the characteristic as it pops up in your own personality.**
- *Be at choice* and *play with options.*

Play with making the characteristic bigger, smaller, or nonexistent. And keep this project all to yourself. It's a personal matter, a secret between you and you, an inner sport, a way to help yourself to a better you. If you have a characteristic you really want to doll up or dampen, you would do well to include it in your practice of positive visualization and positive self-talk. Your primary motive is to expand the space between you and the characteristic so that you can view it with a sense of detachment, and gain the free will to do some creative choreography with your own personality and performance.

Keep in mind that your confining, negative, and/or outdated concepts and behaviors come from a massive number of folks and factors, so for heaven's sake don't waste time seeking out someone to blame—least of all your parents. Parents are easy targets, and too often they get a bad rap. Most parents I've met try their darndest to do right by their kids, and while I'm not sure about your parents' intentions or actions, I know for certain that if you cling to the belief that your shortcomings are their fault or, sillier yet, their responsibility, you won't sink all the way into the fulfillment and contentment you deserve.

As you practice taming your gremlin by *simply noticing, choosing and playing with options,* shining a bright light on old habits and concepts, and experimenting with new behaviors, you will learn, or relearn, perhaps on a deeper level than before, that you are in charge of your life. It's true. Like it or not you are, indeed, in charge. And if that realization has not left you shaking in your boots, then you have not fully had it.

Your Life Is *Your* Life

One way or another we all at some point get hit in the face by a blast of wind, open our eyes, and see that we are not only on the bow of a colossal sailboat on an open sea, but that we're the captain of the damned thing. Once you glimpse this fact of life, you have some choices. You can squeeze your eyes shut and make believe you don't have to take the wheel, you can run around flapping your arms and yelling "Somebody take the wheel, somebody take the wheel," or you can take the wheel and learn to handle it.

If you settle down and trust the wind instead of fearing it, you'll eventually become pretty good at sailing. You will find that while you don't know what's around the next cape, and while you may at times work up a soaking sweat trying to stay afloat in a nasty storm, all in all you can have a fine time sailing where you want to and occasionally you can drop anchor and bask in the sun. The breeze is always blowing, at least a bit, so keep your sails unfurled.

What you do with your life is up to you. It's not up to your mom, your dad, your spouse, your pals, your coach, or your therapist. It's all up to you. Just underneath the fear of being in command of your life is outrageous excitement *about* being in command of it. Best of all is the freedom—the freedom to lead your life your way, testing the waters on your own, getting your very own battle scars, and relishing your own rewards. You may hook up with a sidekick or two in this sea of life, but even those relationships will work best if each of you has a clear sense of ownership of your own life.

So let's review. The first step in the Gremlin-Taming Method is to

Simply notice.

The second step is to

Choose and play with options.

Among the options you can play with are:

Breathe and fully experience
Change for a change
Accent the obvious
Just imagine it
Revisit and re-decide

And here's one more option you can use in combination with any of the above. You've already got it in your arsenal of gremlin-taming tools:

Center yourself, remembering that special place behind your heart and making use of your "I'm taming my gremlin" mantra.

Below is a note from you to you. Have some fun filling in the blanks. In doing so, you'll review most of the key points we've covered so far.

Dear _____
　　　　　(your name)

　　To establish the *here* and n _ _ as your h _ m _ base is a good idea. From this base, you can begin to exercise control over your s p o t _ _ g _ t of a _ _ r e n _ _ s. This will help you *simply notice* not just what is going on around you, but your own habits and the c _ n _ _ p t _ on which they are based. Sometimes the concepts are like a veil between you and your personal experience.

　　Once you simply n _ _ _ c _ an outdated h _ b _ t or concept at play, or hear your gremlin chattering, you will be *at choice* and can then play with o _ t _ _ n _. If you become aware of any habits or concepts that you want to experiment with modifying, you can change for a c h _ n _ e or even have some fun accenting the obvious.

　　As you stroll through life from this point forward, you're going to remember to c _ n t _ _ yourself and use your "I'm taming my gremlin" mantra. It will help you stay centered if you pay

attention to the miraculous s h _ a t h that separates you from all else—your s _ _ n. And it
will be helpful, too, for you to remember that your
b r _ _ _ h _ n g is both a barometer and a regulator of your experience.

Love from your pal,

_____

(Sign here the name by which you most like to be called.)

We've covered a lot of ground together. Whether
your mind has assimilated it all is immaterial. What is
important is that the natural you has time to assimilate
it. For that reason, I'd like to suggest that you take breaks
often as you read this book. Certainly, if you get confused
or distracted, stop reading for a while. We'll continue on
together when you are in the mood. I'm not going any-
where.

9
Common Gremlin
Strategies

Detecting and foiling your gremlin on the spot is always possible but often very challenging. A little bit of knowledge about common gremlin strategies can enhance your awareness. Remember, to *simply notice* him is the first step in taming him.

THE "YOU CAN'T" STRATEGY

This strategy, while crude and unsophisticated, has been a part of the activity of every gremlin I have encountered.

In the "You Can't" strategy, your gremlin convinces you that you are not capable of obtaining certain results by your actions. Your gremlin knows that if you believe you have limits, you will never actualize your potential. If you are unaware of your gremlin, he, of course, has an obvious edge. After all, he has bombarded you with *can'ts* since before you were old enough to reason. You probably accepted them carte blanche, without consideration. You may not even be aware of the *can'ts* you have accepted.

As you begin to become aware of the *can'ts* by which you live your life, you may find that some are accurate: you can't fly, you can't grow taller on the spot, and you can't walk on water. Others, however, may be subtle and very powerful: you can't change, you can't tame your gremlin, you can't build anything with your hands, you can't be a good athlete, you can't survive alone, you can't make money, you can't have a lasting relationship, you can't be an academic success, you can't relax, and you can't stand it (the *it* can take infinite forms). The "I can't stand it" line is a real puzzler. I'm never sure what it means to people using it. Does it mean that they will explode, melt, or disintegrate?

When you hear *can't* or the phrase *I can't* rumbling around in your head, be alert to the possible presence of your gremlin. Breathe and center yourself. Use your "I'm taming my gremlin" mantra. Consider rephrasing the words you have just spoken or thought, replacing *can't* with *won't* or *will* or *will not* with *choose to* or *choose not to*. This will remind you of your responsibility for the limitation and in some cases your ability to remove a limitation.

When you have done this you might consider adding the words "until now" at the end or beginning of the thought or spoken phrase. This phrase is one of the most powerful tools you have for taming your gremlin on the spot. For example, you might change:

I *can't* tell him what I feel.

to

I *choose not* to tell him what I feel.

to

Until *now* I have chosen not to tell him what I feel.

If your choice is to continue to do as you have always done *until now*, that is neither good nor bad. All that is important in this aspect of Gremlin-Taming is that you take responsibility for your choice. Simply notice whether your choice is based on a feared consequence or on a past experience rather than on the present situation

and your desired outcome. If so, you might wish to come out of the world of mind long enough to assess the validity of your fear given the current moment.

Enjoying yourself requires awareness of your freedom of choice, and the words *until now* will put you at the all-important point of *choice*. When you are not in touch with your choice in any given situation, you will tend to feel trapped. Feeling trapped and enjoying your life are hardly compatible states of being. I hope that you opt for enjoying your life.

135

THE "YOU SHOULD," "YOU OUGHT TO," AND "YOU MUST" STRATEGY

We have already discussed this strategy briefly, but let's review it. *Should, must,* and *ought* are gremlin terms. You too may use them on occasion, but your gremlin uses them frequently with the intention of trapping you in a sort of toxic duality.

If you lead your life in total accord with *shoulds, oughts,* and *musts,* it's as if you are a computer programmed with rules that predetermine your responses to feelings and situations. This can lead you to miss entirely the freshness, excitement, and potential for creativity inherent in living.

Your gremlin will use *shoulds, oughts,* and *musts* to trap you into forming a rigid, unconscious dependency on fixed or habitual response. This can actually make you very anxious (sometimes panicky) when you encounter intense and powerful emotions and/or situations for which your *shoulds, musts,* and *oughts* do not seem to apply.

I rushed to Oklahoma City when I got the news of the bombing of the Murrah Building on April 19, 1995. In a matter of hours after the bombing I found myself responding to families of victims, some of whom had gotten bad news; others who were waiting to hear the fate of their loved ones. But one of the most distraught people I dealt with was a man who was trembling uncontrollably. As far as he knew, he had no relatives or acquaintances in the building at the time of the explosion. He was in his late 40s, clean-cut, and wearing an obviously expensive business suit. As I held him and talked with him, it became clear to me that his crisis was engendered not so much by the horrific event that had occurred but by his own reaction to the powerful emotion he experienced when, from his car, he saw the destruction. In other words, his concept of himself did not allow for him to feel the depth of emotion he was experiencing. His concept of himself was as an always-in-charge macho male completely in control of his emotions. His habit for responding to strong emotions of any sort had always been to block them. This habit was based on a firm *should* that *strong men do not cry.*

I helped him manage his emotions by staying in physical contact with him and helping him to allow them to flow, which in this case meant letting himself sob deeply for a very long time. I said to him several times, in several ways, "What you're feeling is as natural as nighttime. Your body is doing what it wants to do. Trust it." I encouraged him to relax his breathing and give his feelings lots of space. Before long he calmed down, and as we talked, he began to understand how his image of manhood, that is to say his concept of who he was and how the world worked, had run head-on into his expressive, naturally deep emotional reaction, and that it was the tension between the two that was causing his shaking. He walked away sad, but no longer shaking, and I believe he learned from the experience.

Simply noticing and playing with options are powerful tools for freeing yourself from your gremlin's outdated *shoulds* and *oughts.* Doing battle with the *shoulds*, *oughts*, and *musts* will lock you into an internal battle with your gremlin, and you've already learned:

When you begin to grapple with your gremlin, he has defeated you.

Precisely what he wants is your attention. As long as you are interacting with him beyond simply noticing him, your energy will not flow freely. It will be tied up in a duality, your life will be much less enjoyable than it could be, and you will feel anything but peace and contentment within. When you hear a *should, must,* or *ought* in your head, consider replacing it in your thoughts and language with a *choose to* or *choose not to.* Again, the idea here is to channel your energy to the *natural you* and away from your gremlin; that is, to place you, yourself, *at choice.*

Being *at choice* will be accompanied by a feeling of excitement (perhaps hidden initially by a veil of fear

and/or feelings of vulnerability) and an increased sense of freedom. You will still have an opportunity to make a choice and, by virtue of that choice, will feel less burdened, trapped, or anxious.

Trusting the *natural you* instead of listening to your gremlin may be a little scary at first. That's natural. But so what? Change for a change. Risk trusting yourself once in a while, just for fun. For goodness' sake, please don't let your gremlin tell you that you should or must change. Sneaky devil that he is, he'll hit you with just such a paradox . . . the old *"you shouldn't have shoulds"* trick.

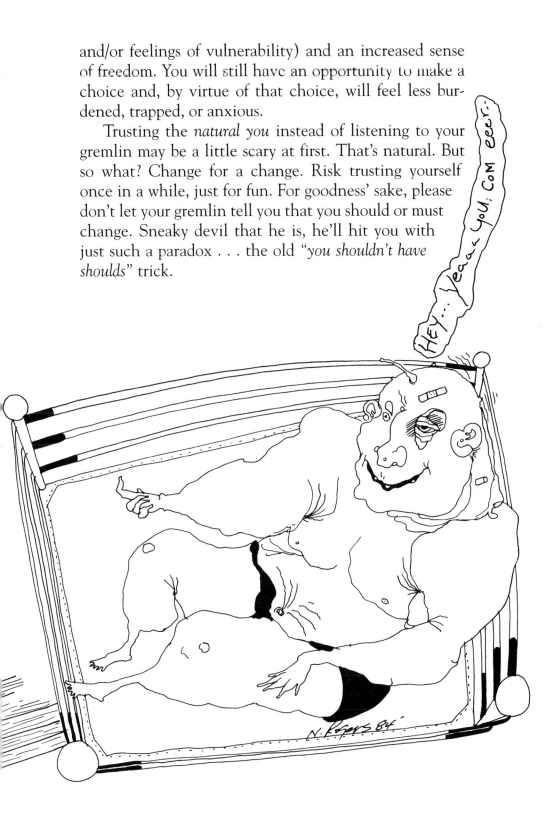

THE "YOU NEED" STRATEGY

When you hear yourself speaking or thinking the word *need*, pay attention. It is true that you need food and water, air, shelter, and love, but most of what you imagine you need you simply want (though in some cases you may want it very badly). Someone, sometime, started the rumor that to tell loved ones that we need them is a compliment. But think for a moment. Would you feel better inside if someone said to you that they really "need" you, or if they said, "I really love you and I want to be with you?" Replacing the word *need* with the word *want* can be a powerful tool in taming your gremlin.

I counsel many couples who believe on a deep level that they need each other. When there is this sort of intense need between people, there is also intense mutual resentment. It is quite beautiful and freeing when these couples begin to recognize the feeling of freedom inherent in *choosing* to be together rather than *needing* to

be together. This slight shift in the flavor of the relationship allows people the space to begin really loving one another.

An image I've had on several occasions when working with couples who were feeling very "needy" is of two cats I loved very much. When my cats Sophie and Jessie were kittens they used to play actively on the floor. Sophie and Jessie looked to me as if they were wrestling. They would place their forepaws on each other's necks as they rolled over and over. In a way it appeared like they were hugging one another, all the while licking and chewing on each other's face. They looked really happy. What I noticed also, however, is that while they were "making nice" and playing with the upper parts of their bodies they were, with their back paws, clawing the daylights out of one another's stomachs. Somehow this image seems appropriate when I encounter couples who think they need each other.

THE "YOU DON'T DESERVE" STRATEGY

In this strategy your gremlin convinces you that you are not worthy of something you want, be it a material thing, a good time, or peace of mind. He will do all in his power to make you feel undeserving, inadequate, afraid, or guilty. Simply remember: guilt serves not one positive purpose. Think of your guilt as an IOU. Either tear it up or ask yourself who it is you owe and what it is you owe them. Make a reasonable decision as to what act, if any, you want to perform in order to allow yourself to tear up the IOU, then perform the act as quickly as possible and tear up the IOU. With your freedom of choice comes responsibility. So remember, you are responsible for your choices.

THE "FANTASY IS REALITY" STRATEGY

Your gremlin loves the idea of having you lead your life based on assumptions. The world of mind is his turf. Sometimes simply taking the time to accurately phrase your processes as you notice them will send your gremlin scurrying and bring you from fantasy into reality, and hence to the all-important point of choice.

If, for example, you feel that your employer will reject an idea that you really want to share with him, you might say to yourself, "I am imagining that my boss will reject my idea." It's important that you emphasize the word *imagine*, for what you are after is a heightened awareness of the way your gremlin is frightening you. In other words, you are simply noticing and accentuating the obvious.

You can explore your fantasy to whatever depth you choose by following this process format and filling in the blanks accordingly.

If I _____
(action #1 you are afraid to take)

I imagine that _____.
(consequence #2)

If _____
(Insert response from #2)

I imagine that _____.
(consequence #3)

If _____
(Insert response from #3)

I imagine that _____.
(consequence #4)

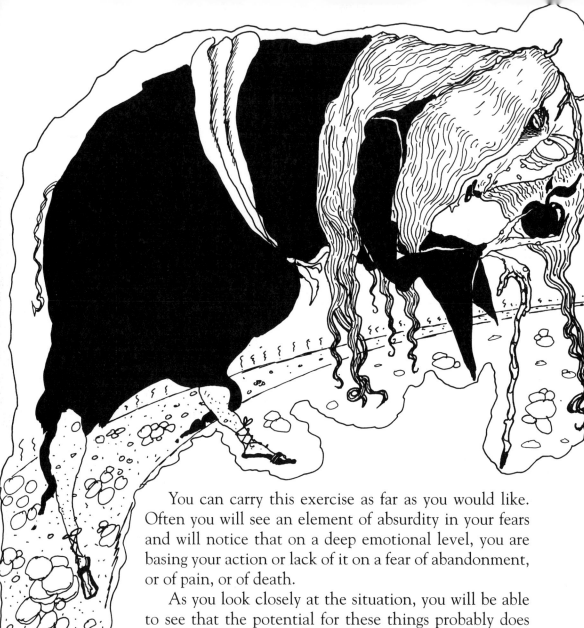

You can carry this exercise as far as you would like. Often you will see an element of absurdity in your fears and will notice that on a deep emotional level, you are basing your action or lack of it on a fear of abandonment, or of pain, or of death.

As you look closely at the situation, you will be able to see that the potential for these things probably does not exist at all. Your gremlin is sly and manipulative. Given almost any circumstance, he can, without your even noticing, transport you to an earlier time when you feared being left or hurt or when it seemed to you that your survival was threatened. He may not taunt you with a conscious memory, but rather with a deep emotional

144

sense of imminent doom. The thought process format I have suggested above will help you *simply notice* and accent the process your gremlin is using to scare you, and will help you to escape the world of make-believe. This will afford you some clarity and perspective from which to choose your action.

Accenting the process your gremlin is using to scare you will diminish the fear. This is related to the Zen Theory of Change we discussed earlier:

I free myself not by trying to be free, but by *simply noticing* how I am imprisoning myself in the very moment I am imprisoning myself.

It may simply be that, like the proverbial child with his hand caught in the cookie jar, your gremlin, once caught, becomes embarrassed and stops what he is doing. Once your fear is diminished, you may still choose not to take a risk. That's fine. But at least your choice will be based on realistic considerations such as timing and real consequences, rather than on an outdated concept or habit formed long ago, or on unrealistic fantasies about the future. A not-so-old adage applies here:

Anxiety is the gap between now and then.

One much overlooked option for determining whether or not to risk a particular action is to test your considerations by stating them aloud. Hearkening back to the example we explored a few pages ago, you might say to your employer, "I have an idea I want to share with you and I'm not sure how open you would be to my suggestion. Would you like to hear it?" Or, "I have an idea I'm considering sharing with you. When and how would be the best way to do that?" Or "I have an idea I'd like to share with you and get your thoughts on. It needs some refinement. I think it might benefit the company in the long run if you will apply your expertise to it."

These sorts of statements are not panaceas, just options. Even thinking them to yourself without verbalizing them often can be very freeing. And remember, don't let your gremlin tell you that you should or must change, or that you should or must take risks. Instead, use the Gremlin-Taming Method:

Simply Notice
Choose and Play with Options
Be in Process

146

THE "TENSING IN ANTICIPATION OF PAIN HELPS" STRATEGY

Several years ago I took a session of rolfing. Rolfing involves very deep massage and can be a painful and intense physical experience. It is a process in which a trained practitioner physically softens and smooths out the connective tissue formed around the body's muscles. During the rolfing session I noticed myself tensing as the rolfer was working very deeply on my abdominal muscles. I feared being hurt. By the same token, I knew that the deeper I could allow the rolfer to work, the more I would benefit from the session. I began to notice my tendency to tense my body in anticipation of pain—rather than in response to the pain itself. I was tensing in an effort to somehow defend myself against pain. This sort of tense preparedness is almost valueless. It is your gremlin that creates the illusion that tensing in anticipation of pain is helpful. Again, the reality is that you can best handle most situations, no matter how complex, if you are relaxed, alert, and centered.

When we are in a state of relaxed concentration, our bodies are more likely to move in fine accordance to the demands made upon them. As I relaxed more, the rolfer was able to work deeper and deeper. When I actually felt pain my body tensed very naturally, but not until the pain actually occurred. My pain and tension were diminished by the end of the session. I enjoyed myself and I benefited a great deal.

Your gremlin wants you to believe that tensing against emotional pain before it occurs will minimize the discomfort. Actually, this does nothing but initiate the discomfort or pain. Pain is no more than tension, so when you tense in anticipation of pain, all you are really doing is beginning

147

the pain early and/or prolonging it. In interpersonal relationships, this sort of defensiveness tends to create and exacerbate unpleasantness and limit the possibility of intimacy. I suppose this dynamic was at play with Sally, me, and my neck.

THE "HEM AND HAW" STRATEGY

When you are bursting to say something but are afraid of the consequences of doing so, your gremlin may encourage you to *hem and haw*. I have had clients whose gremlins have scared them into developing highly sophisticated hem and haw techniques as a way of avoiding the excitement of raw human contact.

One of my clients used an amazing sense of timing, an authoritative voice, sweeping gestures, and phrases such as "sort of," "if you will," and "wouldn't you agree" to get one or more listeners to nod their heads in agreement to his pseudo-intellectual pontification. This method of non-communication comprised, in part, his act of Benevolent Philosopher. I once saw him commandeer an entire dinner party for a solid ten minutes with a spontaneous mini-lecture that, as near as I could tell, didn't make a lick of sense. But he didn't make a lick of sense with a lot of confidence. He said things like, "I found the whole event sort of moribund—Kafkaesque, if you will. Wouldn't you agree?"

The Benevolent Philosopher had many acquaintances but felt that no one really knew him. Had he been at all centered and in touch with himself he would have physically detected his gremlin, for hem-and-hawers often develop a feeling of tightness in their stomachs, an aching head, shortness of breath, and a general feeling of discontent. Also, had he been willing to quit hemming and haw-

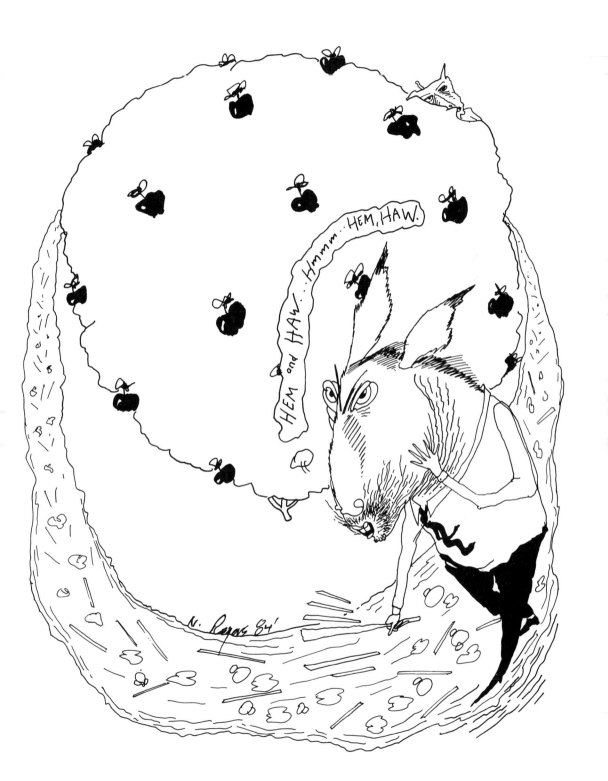

ing long enough to notice he might have seen puzzled looks, people yawning, and fixed, insincere smiles.

But that's the way it is with gremlins. They sneak up on us when we least expect them to and suddenly and secretly trap us into behaviors which, when objectively witnessed, are downright embarrassing.

We, of course, don't know what we don't know. When we are hemming and hawing our gremlin has convinced us to let slide our all-important tools of:

Simply Noticing

Choosing and Playing with Options

Being in Process

Fortunately for us, when we see our gremlin in action we can tame him on the spot.

To be free of the hem and haw strategy, we need only become aware of our wants, our thoughts, and our emotions, and describe them clearly and concisely. A simple sentence is far more powerful than an elaborate analogy or explanation when it comes to making yourself understood and putting your gremlin in his place. If you truly do want to hide yourself rather than express yourself, that is fine. Simply make the choice to do so instead of hemming and hawing.

When you hem and haw or *peek and hide*, as some of my clients have called it, you risk looking foolish. That's probably not what you want, but it is probably what your gremlin wants. Remember, when you are feeling one thing and expressing another, you are being phony. While it is a tough pill to swallow, you and I are just as transparent as everybody else. And phoniness stands out like a sore thumb.

If you want to say something but you are feeling afraid or cautious, mentally acknowledge the consequence you

150

fear and consider stating it (the consequence) aloud. Often, this level of intense honesty will shock your gremlin into a state of temporary immobilization. With your gremlin immobilized, the *fear* of unpredictability will become the *excitement* of unpredictability. You will be in touch with your freedom to say precisely what you mean. Knowing what it is you want to say and saying it clearly and concisely is usually a good idea. Hemming and hawing is good for no one and will seldom get you what you want.

When you communicate clearly and succinctly instead of hemming and hawing, you will feel much more alive and you will open yourself to the possibility of intimacy and warmth in your relationships. When you hem and haw you avoid the potential for the growth and the unpredictability inherent in every human relationship. Your relationships will become predictable, superficial, and, above all, boring.

A relationship is a system and, as with all systems, when there are no new inputs the system enters a state of entropy or degradation. Risk-taking and new inputs into human relationships are essential if the relationship is going to thrive and deepen.

Below are some rules your gremlin would love to have you follow, as he knows they will ensure shallow relationships and perpetual disappointment:

- **Use generalizations such as "we" and the impersonal "you" or "people" instead of the term "I."**
- **Confuse feeling with thinking.**
- **Confuse the world of mind with what's actually going on within you and around you.**
- **Conceptualize problematic situations in such a way as to make others responsible for your misery.**

- Smile when you are angry and sad.
- Use "can't" when you mean "won't."
- Lead your life in accordance with rules and regulations, and without taking into account your natural desires and the current moment and situation.
- Make an effort to keep relationships comfortable and predictable; and, for goodness' sake, don't rock the boat.
- Relate to those close to you as you have always related to them.
- Assume that you know what others are thinking and feeling.
- Never disagree.

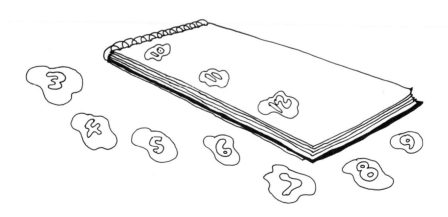

- Be clear about the roles others expect you to play, and make certain not to make them uncomfortable.
- Confuse wants and needs.
- Don't say "no."
- Use lots of filler words such as "know what I mean," "sort of," and "wouldn't you agree."
- Avoid eye contact.
- Interrupt.
- Breathe shallowly and rapidly.
- Instead of listening, think ahead to what you want to say next.
- Tell people what they should and ought to do.

THE "MY FEAR IS SCARING ME TO DEATH" STRATEGY

In this strategy, your gremlin will convince you that you are about to die. This is a cruel and vicious strategy used by gremlins when they are feeling desperate. I once had a client named Hank who had a family history of heart disease. The media had warned him that he was a Type A personality. His anxiety about having a heart attack was tremendous, yet he knew that the last thing he needed was anxiety. He became anxious about his anxiety. The whole cycle perpetuated itself until Hank began to have one anxiety episode after another. These usually took the form of chest pains, shortness of breath, and a shaky feeling within. On several occasions, Hank rushed to the emergency room. He had medical tests and medical workups done, all of which determined that there was nothing wrong with his heart.

In our work together, Hank developed a mechanism for taming his gremlin on the spot. He simply centered himself, used his Gremlin-Taming mantra, and began to *simply notice* his gremlin. He allowed his gremlin five to ten minutes of vicious monologue. He listened to all that his gremlin had to say. Sometimes, he enjoyed playing with the option of accenting the obvious. He did so by verbalizing his gremlin's statements. I asked Hank to take on his gremlin's voice and make a recording for him and me. We played it in my office and in a deep guttural tone a tirade something like this emerged:

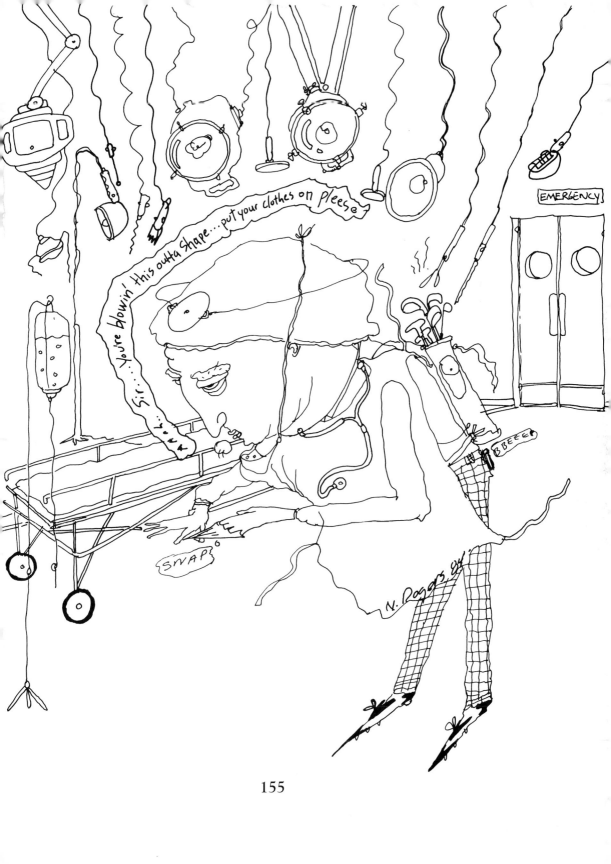

"Well, now you've done it. Boy, your family's sure gonna miss you. You're gonna croak any minute. Look at you! You're a nervous wreck. You're fat. Your breathing is shallow. You're scared to death. You're a wimp, an imposter, and a no-account, and you don't deserve a life. It's all a house of cards, Butterball, and it's about to crumble; and when it does, it's gonna fall right on you. It's all over but the shoutin', Buddy Boy. I can't for the life of me imagine how you've managed to live this long. The only reason you even have a job is because your boss can't see through you. If people in this world really knew you, they'd see that you're just a big, fat baby. You can't keep up this pace forever, Sonny. You're probably gonna lose your job tomorrow, and your wife's getting a little fed up with you anyway. She's probably having an affair right now. And your kids don't like you. They're certainly not proud of you. You're losing control over them and over yourself. You're on your way out and it's not gonna be a graceful exit."

156

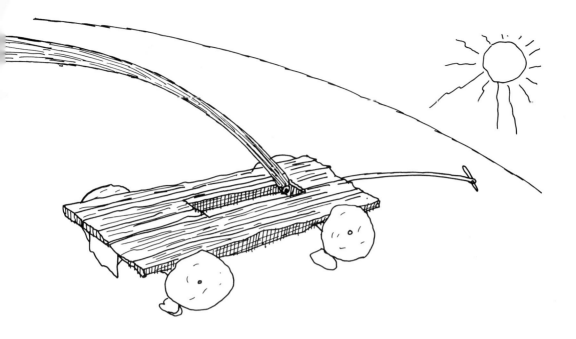

And on, and on, and on. Instead of grappling with his gremlin, Hank, once centered, was able to sit back and simply listen to him, accenting the gremlin's chatter from time to time. He developed a sense of detachment from his gremlin and after a few minutes would simply focus his awareness either on his body or on the world via his sensory receptors, instead of in the world of mind.

This brought Hank to the all-important point of choice. On rare occasions, he decided he wanted to give his gremlin more play. He let himself do so, but he always set a limit in advance on the amount of time he would allow his gremlin to rampage. This rather tight, structured approach to Gremlin-Taming has worked for Hank. It reminds him of the importance of choice and of his ability to relax and focus his awareness wherever he chooses.

If your gremlin is pushing you to a point where your anxiety is scaring you, practice centering, use your Gremlin-Taming mantra and:

Simply Notice

Choose and Play with Options

(Accenting the obvious, perhaps, as Hank did.)

Be in Process

And practice. Practice. Practice. Every gremlin attack is a practice opportunity.

THE "THEY HAVE TO CHANGE IN ORDER FOR ME TO FEEL BETTER" STRATEGY

I recall a crisp, sunny, Saturday morning not long ago, a day in which appreciating the life within was coming easy. I meditated, ran, had a fine breakfast with my wife and son, and got myself ready to drive from my home near Fort Worth to Austin, Texas, to conduct a workshop.

I felt content, free, clear, loving, and wise. Life was a bowl of cherries. There I was, gliding down the highway, listening to the Supremes, when I was abruptly and rudely assaulted by a blaring horn. Even if you have but a rudimentary knowledge of highway etiquette, you are no doubt aware of a honk continuum bounded on the one end by a polite, "I hate to interrupt, but we really must move along now" beep, and on the other by a "move it or lose it" blast that lasts. This blaring intrusion was solidly in the latter category.

My neck muscles grew tight as baseball twine, a reflex action. An attempt to pull my head inside my body, I suppose. My knuckles turned white as my grip on the wheel intensified. My eyes were wide. My skin was tight. Then I saw him. He sped by on my left, guffawed, flipped me off, and leaned on his horn again for good measure

before cutting back in front of me and goosing it.
He seemed to be having a big time at my expense.

He was driving a small truck with huge wheels.
(I have a wild disdain for this type of vehicle. They
remind me of cockroaches.) The driver was young,
skinny, and ugly. His rear window brandished a gun rack
and a rebel flag decal. I did not love this human.

I had been in my own lane, traveling the speed limit,
innocent, thinking pure and noble thoughts, and mind-
ing my own business. In an instant, the blissful feeling I
had relished all morning was kicked aside in favor of a
flash of pure fear, and the fear had hardly settled in
before it was sent tumbling by a passionate urge to maim.

Not only had my life flashed before my eyes, but now
my gremlin had me totally convinced that my manhood
was on the line. Miraculous how fast it had happened. In
two or maybe three seconds, I had been transformed from a
mild-mannered, love-filled, benevolent Saint Francis kind
of guy into a pit-bull dog. I wanted to squash that mini-

truck and chew off the face of its pea-brained driver. I wanted revenge, dammit. My mind squealed, "Make him beg for mercy," and once again the queen bee of gremlin myths had a death grip on my psyche. Ah, I know her well: It was the old "I'll feel at peace again when, and only when, I straighten him/her/them/it out" myth.

I've experienced many variations on this theme, but usually it boils down to the belief that my peace of mind depends on my being proclaimed "right," although I've also been known to hold out for being seen as "righteous," "the best ever," and, in earlier days, "cool." It's a paradoxical stance at best, since it results in my surrendering without a fight to the props and players in my world total power over where I will be placed on the pain/pleasure yardstick of existence.

It's true that, like it or not, circumstances affect my moment-to-moment level of contentment—and yours, too, I'll bet. To be sure, I for one am a devotee of the *if you don't like your circumstances, change them* point of view. But where enjoying this life is concerned, I'm into expediency. I'm an addict, hooked on peace of mind, and an addict will stop at nothing. So maybe, just maybe, I could feel good even if this scum-suckin', truck-driving lowlife sped off into the future without seeing that, on this trail, on this day, I was wearing the white hat and he was a slithering snake in the grass.

Feeling good when your ego has been tweaked isn't easy. On that fateful Saturday I pulled it off (which makes for a dull ending to this tale, I know, but we're here to learn, not just to be entertained, right?). I let that no-account truck driver drift to the background of my experience (so let him drift into yours, please) and settled back into a relative state of calm contentment. It was a small victory, I know. Nothing comparable to illness, divorce, death of a loved one, or famine. But the game is essentially the same.

The Supremes helped. No doubt about it. But not nearly so much as some of the skills we have covered. From over three decades of intimate involvement with individuals, families, and businesses in transition, I've woven these skills into a deceptively simple, practical, step-by-step system for staying calm and at least relatively content even in the midst of upheaval. I call them the Basics of Pleasure. You've learned them and earned them. Use them. All day, every day—especially after a blaring horn. Here they are.

The Basics of Pleasure

1. Make being centered and feeling good a top priority.
2. Remember that doing so is primarily an inside job.
3. Remember where you end and all else begins—that miraculous sheath known as your skin.
4. Breathe, dammit, breathe.
5. Relax your pact to keep your act intact.
6. Establish the *here* and *now* as home base from which you consciously direct your spotlight of awareness.

Blaring horns come in many forms. To tense when you are assaulted by one is natural. But how long you hold onto the tension is up to you. If your gremlin traps you into chewing on the memory of the blaring horn event as if it were bubble gum, your tension and discomfort may last for hours or even days. And it's important to remember that there is rarely a positive correlation between your shaping other people up and your inner peace being restored. Practice the Basics of Pleasure. I think you will find them a powerful alternative.

10

A Quick Review

Remember the *simply* in *simply noticing* and the *playing* in *choosing and playing with options*. Play with filling in the blanks below. It will help you to reflect on what you have learned.

You have learned The Basics of Pleasure. That is, that being c _ n _ _ r _ d is a top priority. Attaining this state of being is primarily, if not exclusively, an i _ s _ d _ job, a job that begins with knowing where you end and all else begins, a miraculous sheath known as your s _ _ n. And you have learned that your breathing is both a barometer and a regulator of your internal experience. You know that a good act is a boon, but you know too that you are not your act, and to relax your pact to keep your act intact will save you a lot of misery.

Having developed the ability to center yourself, you are able to establish the h _ _ _ and n _ _ as a home base from which you regulate your spotlight of a w _ r _ _ e s _. With your spotlight, you are able to s _ m _ l _ n _ t _ _ e your gremlin's chatter as well as the habits and c _ n c _ p _ _ that he perpetuates. You know the importance of attending to your habits for responding to emotions as well as your habits for responding to people and life circumstances. You know how to use

162

your spotlight of awareness to become aware of outdated concepts such as your <u>s</u> _ _ <u>f</u>-concept and your concepts about how the world works. As you become aware of old behaviors and habits, you will be able to choose and <u>p</u> _ _ <u>y</u> with options.

Among your options are:

Breathe and fully experience

Change for a <u>c</u> _ _ _ <u>g</u> _

A <u>c</u> _ _ <u>n</u> _ the obvious

Just _ <u>m</u> <u>a</u> _ _ <u>n</u> _ it

Revisit and re-decide

AND

center yourself, noticing your breath passing over that special place behind your heart and using your mantra of "I'm taming my gremlin"

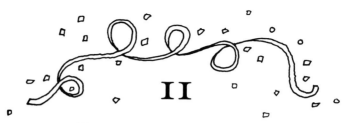

II

Being in Process

Making a conscious decision to see your Gremlin-Taming™ as an ongoing adventure that will be forever in process is an essential part of having a truly satisfying inner experience. There is no finish line when it comes to gremlin-taming. Yet, with practice, you will become so efficient at taming your gremlin® on the spot that even his loudest bullhorn, his most sophisticated strategies, his most low-down shenanigans will become barely a brief annoyance. Your gremlin wants you to believe that your happiness lies somewhere in the future as a reward to be granted once you have arranged your actions and the people and circumstances of your life into the right configuration. As you begin to tame your gremlin, however, you will gain an appreciation for the simple truth that contentment is not a static state—not an entity to be captured. Rather, it is an experience that, like misery, is available and accessible within you.

Being in process is an attitude—an appreciation of this simple truth and of the reality that your life will be forever unfolding and your future always unknown. Allowing yourself to acknowledge that this is so might be unsettling, but as you practice and move toward mastery of the Gremlin-Taming Method, this fact of life will become not only palatable but invigorating. Seeing yourself as *in process* will help you increase your level of simple moment-to-moment contentment and your appreciation of your very own gift of life.

Simply noticing, *choosing and playing with options*, and *being in process* are states of being that are available to you from moment to moment. You will never tame your gremlin forever, be miserable forever, or ensure your happiness forever. In every moment, you have a choice: to heed the words of your gremlin or to be in harmony with the essence of who you really are. *Simply noticing*, *choosing and playing with options*, and *being in process* will help immensely, as will practicing the Basics of Pleasure, centering yourself, and using your "I'm taming my gremlin" mantra.

The choice is yours, moment to moment, breath to breath. Taming your gremlin and enjoying yourself and your life is an ongoing, moment-to-moment process.

12

Just for Kicks

As I've mentioned, gremlins change their styles, appearances, methods, and even their gender from time to time. With that recognition and just for kicks, you might want to do a rough sketch of your gremlin as you imagine him or her at this moment. What does he/she look like? Has she/he a color? Is she/he large or small, slim or heavy, mean-looking, amorphous, distinct?

Play with creating a visual representation of your gremlin. Or write an introduction for him or her. How about a character description as if for a screenplay? Or a job description? Does he remind you of Coach Don Ledup, the Artist, Reverend Al Drydup, or any of the other gremlins I described earlier? Your gremlin might even remind you of someone you know or have known. Or your gremlin may resemble an animal or an object—a dark cloud, perhaps, or a fog. Give him or her a name if you wish. Remember that gremlins change their style and form rather often.

A sketch or written introduction from time to time might be a good idea. If you're unable to visualize your gremlin, that's fine, don't fret. Relax.

On our Web site at the Gremlin Taming Institute™ (www.tamingyourgremlin.com), we have a gallery of gremlins. Send yours along if you'd like it included.

Your relationship with your gremlin will be a lifelong one. Start now to acknowledge him fully, remembering that acknowledgment and entanglement are not the same. *Simply notice* him and the habits for responding to emotions and people by which he insists you lead your life. Notice the concepts on which these habits are based, and notice, too, the effect of your gremlin's presence on your body, your relationships, and, of course, on your overall level of contentment.

Practice and rely on the Gremlin-Taming Method:

Simply Notice
Choose and Play with Options
Be in Process

13

The Essence of It All: True Love

There is your gremlin. And there is the *natural you*. The essence of the *natural you* has many names, none of which can circle it. Earlier we called it *life*, your life. Another term I've often used for it is *true love*.

No description of the experience of true love can do justice to its glory. True love is both subtly and powerfully perfect. True love is not a thought (though certainly you can have loving thoughts). True love is an experience. True love is trustworthy. Just as the sun is always shining whether you can see it or not, true love exists within you always, whether or not you are attentive to it.

When true love comes into your awareness, it permeates your experience and you feel content, peaceful, and satisfied.

The experience of true love is always available to you, though I'll be the first to admit it is easier to tap into and enjoy under some circumstances than others. Getting that sliver of light between you and your gremlin certainly helps.

Experiencing true love does not require something or someone to love—though you may feel true love inside yourself in the presence of certain people and things. Nor do you ensure yourself a large dose of true love by smiling a lot, talking softly, or hugging people with whom you'd rather just shake hands and say hello.

As you learn to tame your gremlin and to tap into and enjoy your experience of the *natural you,* you are going to become increasingly able to detect what configurations of props and players make it easier for you *to* tap into that love. With your gremlin out of the way, the *natural you* will guide you toward experiences that stimulate the love and away from experiences that don't. The true love within you can help you select whom to hang out with, what props and players to surround yourself with, and what activities to engage in.

The experience of true love differs from the experience of excitement, sexual feeling, adoration, or desire, though these pleasurable sensations increase in lip-smacking intensity when laced with or founded upon true love. Pleasurable stimulation can be thrilling; ask your taste buds or your genitals. But even a first-class titillating tingle remains only pleasurable stimulation until you are awakened to the experience of true love lying in a half-sleep behind your heart. Add to that pleasurable stimulation one small full-bodied drop of pure love, and you're in for a real treat.

True love is not an emotion, but it underlies many emotions. True love is more fundamental than emotion. True love is not a wave; true love is the water. It provides you with more than gratifying stimulation. True love fulfills you.

14

From Me to You:
Here and Now

The payoff for me in writing this book has been my enjoyment of the process. The process has included some vague fantasies of future recognition, money, and security, so I know that my gremlin is on the scene—just waiting to hypnotize me into confusing desires with expectations. Sneaky little bastard. He's so persistent. Yet, I don't fear him. Something very beautiful is happening in my life as I spend more time in tune with the *natural me* instead of with him. Simply having that as my intention leaves me feeling enormously satisfied. Increasingly, I'm more in touch with the *natural me* and with the true love that is the essence of us all. I feel it at this moment. Often I have this feeling when I'm speaking or writing from my heart. I like it very much.

Serving this love feels good, and we all have the opportunity to serve it in two ways. First, you can serve it up in the same way you would serve someone a luscious piece of apple pie; that is, you can allow the experience of the *natural you* and the love that is the essence of the *natural you* to be reflected in your words and actions.

Second, you can serve this love as you would a master; that is, respond to it, let it guide you. It will tell you what to say, what to do, whom to hang with, and more. Writing this book feels like serving love to me, and it's the best feeling I know.

Taming my gremlin and becoming more in tune with
my essence is the main event of my life. It's a breath-to-
breath hobby.

No doubt about it, we can all have the ultimately
beautiful inner experience of being alive. It's available.
And it's not a catharsis, not a satori, not a whammo of an
insight, not a hallucinogenic flash, not a Zen moment,
not even a religious revelation, but a pure and constant
readily available experience of our purest essence. And
you don't have to be a swami, an avatar, religious, or hip
and cool in order to pull it off.

As for me, as I've mentioned, I am as much a student as
a teacher of Gremlin-Taming. *Taming Your Gremlin* is my

way of offering some of what I've learned. There are plenty of things I am not confident of in this life, but I am completely confident in this process. It has never let me down.

Should you continue to pursue the pleasure of taming your gremlin, enjoying the *natural you*, and tapping into the true love within you, I would enjoy hearing from you. You may contact me through the Gremlin Taming Institute Web site, www.tamingyourgremlin.com.

My heartfelt desire is that gremlin-taming will prove to be a stepping-stone on your path to the *natural you* and to the true love that is your essence.

Share your experience with others. And above all, enjoy your life.